Country Decorating

What we now refer to as 'country style' is not so much a mode of decorating as a way of life. Country style is not a look that one pays an interior decorator to produce. *Country Decorating* is the result of a whole approach to life which delights in lavishing love and care on creating a comfortable home; a return to the much-maligned practice of homemaking.

Whether quilting, embroidery, folk art and decorative painting or cross stitch is your favourite craft, *Country Decorating* includes projects to delight everyone. Cushions, bed quilts, tea-cosies and plant pots are featured in this comprehensive book.

Country Decorating provides beautiful colour photographs, clear instructions and patterns. A range of projects are included to delight and inspire everyone interested in creating a beautiful country home.

Country Decorating

A Craftworld Book

Craftworld Books Pty Ltd
50 Silverwater Rd
Silverwater NSW 2128
Australia

First published by Craftworld Books Pty Ltd 1999

Managing Editor: Sue Aiken
Editor: Maggie Aldhamland
Associate Editors: Marnie McLean, Karen Winfield
Production Assistant: Jane Richardson
Concept: Vivien Valk Design
Designer: ilash art
Illustrator: Annette Tamone

National Library of Australia Cataloguing-in-publication data

Country Decorating.

Includes index.
ISBN 1 876490 04 7.

1. House furnishings. 2. Needlework – Patterns. 3.
Interior decoration. 4. Decoration and ornament, Rustic.
(Series : Australian country craft series).

746.9

Craftworld Books
Country Decorating

ISBN 1 876490 04 7

Printed by KHL Printing Co. Pte Ltd, Singapore

THE AUSTRALIAN
Country
CRAFT
SERIES
PRESENTS

Country Decorating

Craftworld Books

Contents

Cottage Industry

Restored Treasures

Creative Instincts

Full Bloom

Acknowledgments

DARALYNN BELL
Sunflower Surprise

A florist for many years, Daralynn enjoys the challenge of creating 'something different'. Her considerable talents are evident in her arrangements of long-lasting native flowers and unusual plants. She is keen to encourage others to use our native flora in their floral arrangements.

ROBYN BROOKS
Gold Lace and Pansies

Robyn lives and breathes her art and this is reflected in her home which is filled with beautifully crafted objects and furniture. This artist finds it hard to tear herself away from painting, and even when on holiday overseas Robyn seeks out opportunities to learn new skills and collect new patterns.

DEBBIE CAMPBELL
Jessica's Dressing Table Set

Debbie is primarily a folk artist who has developed her own style of painting which she combines with other crafts, such as needlework and floral decorating. Her needlework has a painterly feel to it and is often inspired by the old or interesting objects she collects.

GARY CLARKE
Fuchsia and Violets

Gary's embroidery is so fine that people often think it has been sewn by machine. He views the art of embroidery as painting with thread and goes far beyond traditional techniques to experiment with stitches and the use of cottons. Gary spends most of his days creating designs and his evenings embroidering them to make sure they work.

THERESIA COOKSON
Country Mouse

Dough modelling has been a part of Theresia's life for many years. Theresia's love of the craft began with the figures she uses to make with her young sons on rainy days in the Netherlands. Later her family migrated to Australia and Theresia found her dough modelling eased the loneliness and isolation she felt during the early years in her new country. Typical of Theresia's style are the little dressed up mice, originally inspired by drawings on a calendar which caught her eye. These days she is constantly creating new characters.

KATE COOMBE
Cottage Garden

Since mastering the traditional American and European styles of folk art, Kate has experimented with many different styles and has pioneered a 'cottage garden' style with a free approach to brush work and paint. Kate creates her own designs and teaches people the skills of folk art.

AVRIL DOBEL
Floral Keepsake

Avril first started pressing flowers to make greeting cards. Since then she has created floral designs for small frames and lids of boxes, as well as larger pieces. She grows many of her own flowers and uses both Australian native flowers and introduced flowers. Avril believes that careful selection of flowers — taking into account aspects of colour, shape, size and texture — is as important as their placement within the design.

JANET DONELLY
Temari Treasure

While living in Japan, Janet learned the ancient craft of Temari — the art of making decorative thread-covered balls — as well as many other traditional paper crafts. Since returning to Australia, Janet has adapted these crafts to suit local conditions by using non-traditional colour combinations. Janet passes on her skills as a teacher, through classes where she concentrates on quick projects such as paper craft coasters, boxes and hanging ornaments, and temari baubles and eggs.

VIVIENNE GARFORTH
Home-made Happiness

Vivienne has been embroidering since she was a child and has won prizes for both creative and traditional embroidery. Vivienne designs pieces with Australian themes, and old family photos and memorabilia often feature in her work. She has also explored découpage, again using Australian images.

NARELLE GRIEVE
Pinwheel and Star Quilt

Narelle prefers hand-quilting to machine quilting as she finds it is more relaxing. Narelle is particularly fond of whole-cloth quilts made from silk and loves the effects of hand-sewing, especially on shiny fabrics which show up the light and shade in the quilting. Narelle is involved in quilting at many levels — as a teacher, writer and judge and is a past president of the Quilters' Guild Inc.

MEREDITH HARMER
Tea for Two

Whenever Meredith moves to a new home, she sets about decorating it with soft furnishings she makes herself. Fabric is what inspires Meredith and she loves to experiment with styles, colours and textures. She believes anyone can make soft furnishings — all that is needed is the ability to sew a straight seam, confidence in handling large pieces of fabric, and a decent sewing machine.

JENNY HASKINS
Sweet Dreams
Doily Drama

Jenny turned her hobby into a profession and has achieved international recognition for her creative sewing. Originally a painter, she loves the three-dimensional aspect of sewing and finds creating works of art that you can use or wear very satisfying. She conducts workshops and demonstrations on machine embroidery techniques in Australia and overseas.

PHYLL HILL
Fancy Glass

In her younger years Phyll studied drawing and oil painting and now uses her skills in decorative painting. Although she still prefers working with oils, Phyll appreciates the convenience of acrylics in folk art. She has broken away from traditional folk art by using more realistic subjects. This multi-talented craftswoman is also expert at découpage, quilting, embroidery and lead lighting.

ROS JENKE
Wildberry Canisters

Ros has won many prizes for her skills in traditional styles of folk art. She creates her own patterns and, with the beginner in mind, includes clear directions and good colour pictures. She has teamed up with fellow artist Lee Dobson to decorate private homes and commercial premises. Ros also uses folk art motifs on quilts and combines her talent as a calligrapher and folk artist to produce sayings on hand-made paper.

SUSAN KAROLY AND ANNIE LONDON
Summer Rose

Quilt maker Susan Karoly and graphic artist Annie London have blended their

skills to develop a new form of trapunto using colour and an easier technique than is used in traditional trapunto. This creative team devise their own designs which they say can be made even by a beginner needleworker.

TITA LEACH
Fairy Quilt

Tita often finds clever ways to combine patchwork and quilting. Her designs are often pictorial, colourful and childlike. Tita prefers hand-quilting to machine-quilting as it gives her a closeness to her creation. She enjoys helping her students to develop their skills and loves the social aspects of sewing together.

SANDRA LEVY
Golden Moments

Sandra is a prolific and creative craftswoman who practises theorem (stencil painting on velvet), and makes grained timber frames, oil floorcloths, patchwork quilts and baskets. She also teaches scherenschnitte (paper cutting) — a craft not well known in Australia. Sandra happily combines a busy family life with her love and enthusiasm for creating craft.

HEATHER LOWNDS
Tulip Planter Box
Floral Topiary

This folk and decorative artist is well known for her pen and wash designs. She believes that folk art allows great creativity in the use of different colours, designs and mediums. Heather teaches her students that anyone can do folk art if they practise. She still attends lessons herself as she finds that there is always something new to learn.

MARILYN MCCANN
Weighty Matters

Decorative painter Marilyn McCann says her expertise is due to daily practice and the exploration of many techniques, styles and mediums. She paints a wide range of things from country scenes to teddy bears and has designed a collection of naive country and urban scenes with an Australian flavour. Marilyn's natural enthusiasm and generous teaching style, has attracted a devoted group of students to her classes.

VAL MOORE
Australian Bush Wreath

A quilter with a great eye for colour and detail, Val teaches her students to assess fabrics for appliqué by cutting a peephole from paper and moving it over material to find a suitable area of colour. Val finds meeting with other quilters inspirational and fun and takes groups of quilters on tours of quilting centres in the USA.

LISA MORANDIN
Seaside Memories

Lisa has had a passion for flowers since an early age so it was natural that she should become a florist. These days she likes to incorporate other objects, such as fruit and vegetables, into her arrangements and also uses silk and dried flowers for longer-lasting effects. Lisa pays particular attention to colour and texture, grouping individual items to give a balanced, harmonious look.

MARY NAYLOR
Felted Mouse

Fibre artist Mary Naylor creates wearable art out of felt and has won many awards at fashion shows. Her work is inspired by the texture and colour of a fleece and by the colours of the Australian outback. Mary teaches people to create practical pieces of clothing as well as craft objects such as pincushions, felt sculptures, bookmarks and brooches.

HELAN PEARCE
Country Garden Cushion

Helan teaches embroidery and likes to create something new and different for each session, maybe a baby blanket with lambs or a piece with flowers. Helan often gains her inspiration from nature and spends a lot of time matching colours. She is always experimenting and developing new techniques to achieve the look she wants.

DIANNE RATCLIFFE
Table of Tuscan Lemons

Ceramics is a constantly changing medium, and it is this flexibility that inspires ceramic artist Diane Ratcliffe. Working closely with fellow artist, Trace Pask in their Brisbane studio, Diane knows no boundaries as she explores new techniques and ideas with great enthusiasm. She believes that the products available today mean that anyone with an interest is able to create quality ceramic art. Dianes creations have largely been inspired by work produced in Europe and the USA.

AUDREY RAYMOND
3-D Effects

What fascinated Audrey Raymond about découpage was the 'cleverness' of it — the fact that you could create something beautiful and original just by cutting out paper images. Competent in many techniques, Audrey's preference is for traditional découpage and she likes to decorate small items such as tiny boxes, miniatures, and even sea shells. Audrey's greatest satisfaction comes from the interaction and exchange of ideas that occurs in her classes. She experiences a great sense of satisfaction from passing on her knowledge as a teacher.

SUE STROM
A Touch of Gold

Sue Strom lists her main loves in life as lace, heirloom sewing and the fashions and lifestyles of people from days gone by, particularly those of the Victorian era. Sue creates her own embroidery designs for soft furnishings and clothing. She constructs delicately embroidered garments partly by machine and partly by hand, although she believes fine materials and French laces deserve the respect of hand-made care.

Introduction

Most of us spend thought, time and effort making our homes welcoming — both for ourselves and our guests. We surround ourselves with beautiful things that reveal our personalities to anyone sensitive enough to read the signs. Many of us include handcrafted treasures to bring a touch of humanity and warmth to our surroundings, and there are few activities more satisfying than making and displaying our own creations.

In this book we present projects that reflect the very best of a variety of crafts, all influenced by the country style. These include appliqué, folk art, quilting and stencilling and less well known crafts such as bread-dough modelling and shadow trapunto. Some of our projects are very simple and will serve as an excellent introduction to the craft while others are examples of the fine work that can be achieved by experienced practitioners. By including such a range of projects we hope that our book will appeal to all who love and admire fine handcrafts, whatever their experience and level of skill.

This book is divided into four theme sections, each containing a selection of different crafts. As some of the crafts featured may be new to you, we have also included a section at the back of the book that explains the basic techniques of many of the crafts featured in the projects.

SECTION 1:
COTTAGE INDUSTRY

The eight projects in this section reflect the simplicity and harmony we have come to associate with the country lifestyle. Some of the projects depict the abundance of the land, while others are reminiscent of the thrift and industry of cottage crafts. Among the crafts featured are stencilling, rag-rug making, appliqué, folk art, cross-stitch, bread dough modelling and quilt making. The crafts featured are suitable for both beginners and experienced craft artists.

SECTION 2:
RESTORED TREASURES

Thrift and concern for the environment are the motivations behind these projects. Pre-used items or objects from nature that cost little or nothing to acquire, can be recycled into fabulous, decorative (and often practical) pieces which will brighten up the home. Among the crafts featured are floral art, folk art, seashell decoration, machine embroidery and quilt making.

SECTION 3:
CREATIVE INSTINCTS

Once the techniques and skills involved in these projects are mastered, they can easily be used in the design of your own creations. The projects in this section are among the simplest to make and include stencilling, embroidery, appliqué, felt making, découpage, machine embroidery and the Japanese craft of temari.

SECTION 4:
FULL BLOOM

All projects in this section contain a floral motif. The flowers used range from Australian native flowers to more traditional favourites like violets and roses. Several of these projects are among the most complicated — and spectacular — in this book. Crafts featured include gold leaf work, folk art, cross-stitch, floral art, shadow trapunto and appliqué.

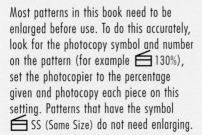

ENLARGING
THE PATTERNS

Most patterns in this book need to be enlarged before use. To do this accurately, look for the photocopy symbol and number on the pattern (for example ▭130%), set the photocopier to the percentage given and photocopy each piece on this setting. Patterns that have the symbol ▭ SS (Same Size) do not need enlarging.

A Brief History

Most crafts practised today have a long history, with some dating back to several centuries BC. Many crafts were developed as practical solutions to everyday problems, such as how to keep warm or how to store food. They also played an important role in satisfying the needs of human beings to create and surround themselves with things of beauty. As you craft your own beautiful objects, it is gratifying to know you are continuing the traditions of a long line of artists and craftspeople from many countries.

We have space here for no more than a brief history of some of the crafts featured in this book, but if you are interested in the origins of a particular craft, you will find books on the subject in your local library.

SCRAP QUILTS

Today's scrap quilts follow the traditions of the early American pioneers. Their quilts were born out of necessity in a time when fabric was scarce and not generally purchased for the sole reason of making a quilt. Housewives kept scrap bags, accumulating scraps of fabric by painstakingly cutting the good parts from worn-out clothes and by saving pieces of fabric left over from sewing garments. Despite the fact that great quilts were made from leftover scraps, care was taken with design and colour. Often fabrics were traded between quilters, until just the right pieces were collected for a certain design.

By the 1850s fabrics were more available as well as less expensive and people began to buy fabric specifically for quilt making. Though they often copied designs handed down from mothers and grandmothers, the availability and wider choice of fabrics allowed them to also create new designs.

Quilts are often associated with sharing — in both giving quilts as gifts and in creating a quilt with others in a marathon quilting bee. The charm and beauty of scrap quilts arises not only from the way the fabrics and design are used, but in the memories that can be associated with every scrap of fabric that is used in making them.

A modern trapunto quilt incorporating shadow work.

TRAPUNTO

While the techniques for working trapunto are simple, the results are glorious and can be quite complex. The idea is to create a relief surface using the effects of light and shadow. Traditionally, trapunto was worked on plain fabric, usually white or cream. Two layers of fabric are used. The pattern is drawn on the lining fabric and then outlined in running stitch to join both layers of fabric together and to completely enclose each section of the design. The threads of the loosely woven line are then eased apart and small pieces of soft wool inserted. When the cavity is filled the threads are moved back together again. In this manner, each small section of the pattern is raised by the padding.

While quilting dates back as far as 3000 BC, trapunto appears to be a more recent form of decoration — created not to provide warmth, but as a means of depicting a story, scene or a design. The earliest known examples of trapunto are three Sicilian wall-hangings made in about 1392 as a wedding gift for two Sicilian aristocrats.

By the 1500s trapunto had spread all over Europe, and was particularly popular in Germany and England. Between the 1500s and the mid-1700s, the wealthy wore glorious gowns and caps decorated with intricate trapunto made by professional workshops. As trapunto went out of fashion in England, its popularity rose in America. Counterpanes made in the trapunto style reached a peak in popularity between 1830 and 1850.

Trapunto is one of the many crafts that has been revived in the latter part of the 20th century. As well as being used to create modern wall-hangings, trapunto is still used in the traditional manner to produce wonderful textile works of art. Many modern examples of trapunto

A traditional-style Baltimore quilt, made by Hitomi Fujita.

incorporate subtle colouring into the design by drawing yarn under the top layer of fabric.

APPLIQUE

Appliqué — the art of stitching one piece of fabric onto another to create simple designs or complex fabric pictures — can be traced back to several centuries BC, when it was used as decoration on animal hide and bark cloth. In the Middle Ages, it was used to stitch heraldic symbols on to knightly accoutrements.

In the 19th century, American quilt makers began using appliqué designs based on traditional German motifs, such as eight-lobed rosettes and three flowers in a pot, and these patterns determined the style of American quilts for the rest of the century. Appliqué reached its height in popularity with the Baltimore album quilt. Still regarded as the quintessential appliqué showcase, these quilts are extremely labour intensive.

In the 1990s, modern sewing accessories have given appliqué a wider appeal. While the intricacy of almost invisible hand-stitching is still regarded as true appliqué, the applied effect can be achieved with iron-on fusible webbing and mock stitching with a permanent marking pen. For machine quilters, there are a variety of stitches available on today's sewing machines to achieve an appliqué finish in a shorter space of time than is possible with hand appliqué.

Theorems are created from a series of numbered stencils.

velvet. In the late 1700s, English migrants to North America took their favourite crafts, including theorem, with them.

In the colonies, theorem painting rapidly became a popular craft both at home and in schools. Indeed, up to the mid-1800s most fashionable ladies' academies on America's eastern seaboard included the craft in their curriculum. Students were given identical still-life design kits containing pre-cut stencils which, by using different placements of stencils and a variety of colour changes, would produce very individual works of art. The homely symbols of abundance — a basket overflowing with fruit or a vase of beautifully arranged flowers — were stencilled in water colours or oils, on fabric as well as paper.

No examples of early Australian theorem painting have been found, but interest in this craft is now growing rapidly in this country.

THEOREM

Theorem is a painting, on paper or creamy velvet or velveteen, created with the aid of stencils. The subject matter is generally a still life, such as a bowl of fruit or a vase of flowers. Only very simple landscapes are ever created because of the difficulty inherent in creating complex stencils. The term 'theorem' stems from the logical method of preparing and numbering the stencils required to create the painting.

Theorem painting is believed to have originated in China or India where the first stencilled paintings were probably done on a kind of rice paper which resembled velvet. Later the technique found its way over to England where theorem designs were first painted on

FOLK ART

Folk art, or the 'art of the people' has its origins in 15th and 16th century Europe. In rural areas of Germany, Austria and Switzerland, wooden furniture was decorated with a style called Bauernmalerei, meaning 'farmer painting', despite the fact that very few farmers actually did it. Mainly local cabinet makers and carpenters made basic furniture, such as cradles, tables, chairs and linen chests, and decorated them, often with the help of other family members, in the long winter evenings. They used paints and stains made from readily available materials such as black soot, white lime and plants. These artisans, who had no formal training, imitated the fine furniture and decorations in castles and churches, and in the homes of the nobility. They took their inspiration from flowers and trees and other objects in their immediate environment, as well as copying the more formal symbols of the church.

Early wooden pieces were stained, not painted, as woodworm was prevalent in Europe, and in some areas it was illegal to cover furniture with paint that might conceal the pests' holes. By the 18th century, however, wood was fully painted and different styles began to emerge over time and in different countries.

Folk art soon extended beyond the painting of furniture. In Austria and Switzerland, entire houses were decorated in the Bauernmalerei style. The Dutch Delftware and the French Limoge porcelain, both have their origins in their countries' folk art traditions. The English were fond of decorative wooden

plates, and canal boat people painted their barges in the folk art style. In America, German and French settlers brought their techniques with them and established the folk art tradition there. In recent years, Australian wildflowers have become popular in local folk art. Some beautifully stylised designs are evolving that combine traditional techniques with images reflecting our own environment.

CROSS-STITCH

Because of the perishability of natural fibres, it is difficult to trace the origins of cross-stitch embroidery. It may have

originated in Egypt in the 7th century, but as it also flourished in China during the Tang dynasty between 618 AD and 900 AD, there are two possible interpretations. Perhaps the craft originated in China and spread via India and Egypt to ancient Greece and Rome, and from there through the eastern Mediterranean and the Middle East. Or it possibly spread in the opposite direction from the Middle East via the silk routes, to China. What is certain, however, is that cross-stitch designs and techniques spread from many of these countries to Europe.

Samplers are particularly important in the history of cross-stitch. The word sampler, comes from the old French word, 'enssamplaire' which means a pattern that can be copied. The earliest dated English sampler in existence was probably worked in 1598 by a Jane Bostocke, to commemorate the birth of a baby, probably her sister. Early samplers were worked in a variety of stitches as well as cross-stitch, but 18th and 19th century examples were worked mainly in cross-stitch, and were used to teach the alphabet and numbers as well as stitchery.

In the 1920s, a cross-stitch revival took place with the establishment of the Danish Cross-Stitch Guild, an organisation that continues to be a source of encouragement for new designers, and whose techniques and patterns are well known all over the world. Today cross-stitch is used to decorate fabric throughout the world, with some of the best examples coming from Eastern European countries, where clothes and household linen have been decorated with this form of craft for hundreds of years.

This tray was inspired by examples of folk art in the small Russian village of Zhostovo.

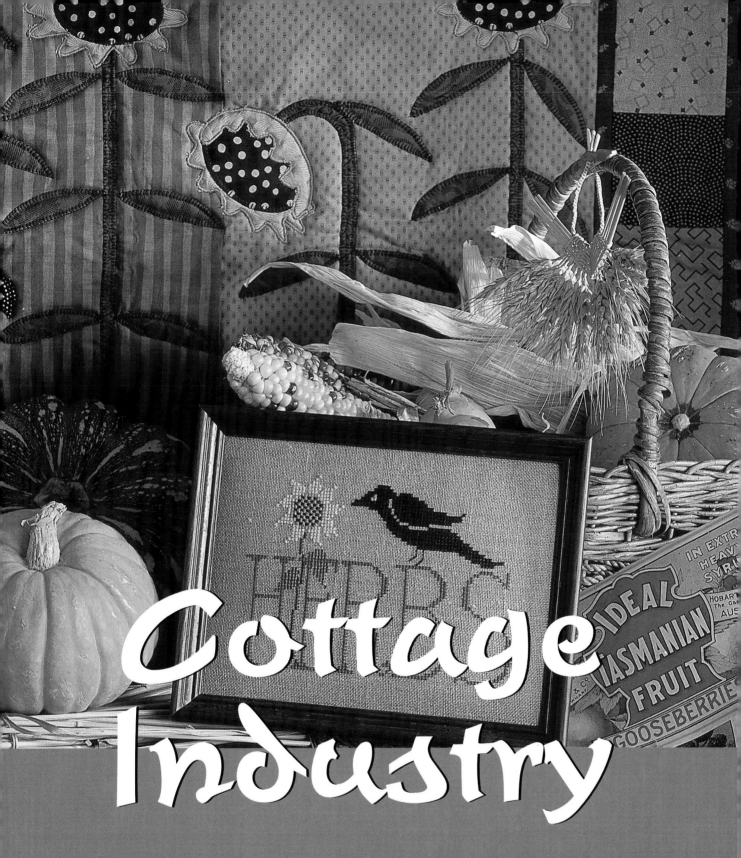

Cottage Industry

At the heart of country craft are visions of cosy farmyard cottages, home baking and abundant harvests. This section carries this happy theme through a variety of crafts, suitable for both beginners through to more experienced craftmakers.

Golden Moments

*A popular pastime among working people for centuries, theorem
painting is the art of stencilling images onto creamy velvet or paper.
Typically, designs contain symbols of abundance and country life.
For this project we provide stencils and instructions for two designs.*

COUNTRY PEAR TREE THEOREM

PREPARATION

Spray the cardboard lightly on one side with spray adhesive. Ensure that the nap of the velveteen is running downwards, so that when you run your hand down the velveteen it feels smooth. Position the cardboard sprayed-side down, onto the centre of the back of the velveteen, and use your hand to smooth it down. Wrap the velveteen edges over the back of the cardboard. Glue the edges down with craft glue and put aside.

CUTTING THE STENCILS

Tape the pattern onto your work surface, then tape a sheet of acetate on top of the pattern. With the felt-tip pen, carefully trace all No 1 outlines onto the acetate, including the centring lines on each edge, and number the top of the sheet as No 1. Repeat the process on the second and third sheets, numbering the top of the sheets as you go.

Place acetate sheet No 1 on the cutting mat and use the craft knife to carefully and accurately cut out the shapes as marked, keeping to the outside of the line. Cut sheets 2 and 3 in the same manner. To avoid

discolouring the paint colours when stencilling, clean any remaining black outlines on the acetate, using a cloth and methylated spirits.

STENCILLING THE PEAR TREE

With the nap running downwards, tape the corners of the velveteen-covered card to the work surface being careful to catch only the edges of the velveteen. Centre sheet No 1 on top of the velveteen, using the centre markers on the stencil, and tape it down. Alternatively, place weights on the stencil to secure it in place.

Squeeze a dab of each colour onto the palette. Dip the stencil brush into the paint and use a circular motion to work the excess paint off onto the palette, before starting to paint. As this is a dry painting method, never go straight from the paint palette to the velveteen without working off the excess paint. If the paint is applied too heavily it will not blend into the velveteen. Instead, dab lightly and build up the colour as you continue. Stencil the pattern onto the velveteen with the relevant colours. Complete sheet No 1 and repeat for each stencil sheet.

The tree trunk is Burnt Umber with a touch of Oxide of Chromium Green, the pears Cadmium Yellow with some touches of Alizarin Crimson and Oxide of Chromium Green. Use Oxide of Chromium Green for the leaves and Alizarin Crimson for the tips. The grass is also Oxide of Chromium

FINISHED SIZE

- Pear tree – 20cm x 25cm (8in x 10in); Country house – 15cm x 20cm (6in x 8in)

MATERIALS

- Spray adhesive
- Craft glue
- Masking tape
- Craft knife and cutting mat
- Paint palette
- Fine black, permanent felt-tip pen
- Methylated spirits and cloth
- 4 small, soft stencil brushes
- No 1 liner brush
- Gum turps
- General sewing requirements

COUNTRY PEAR TREE THEOREM

- 20cm x 25cm (8in x 10in) white, acid-free cardboard
- 30cm x 25cm (12in x10in) white cotton velveteen
- 3 sheets of A4 0.004 acetate film
- Archival Oil Paints: Burnt Umber, Oxide of Chromium Green, Cadmium Yellow, Alizarin Crimson

COUNTRY HOUSE FRAME

- 20cm x 25cm (8in x 10in) pine frame
- Fine sandpaper
- Shellac
- Brush to apply shellac
- 1 sheet of A4 0.004 acetate film
- Masking tape
- Soft varnishing brush
- Jo Sonja's Artists' Acrylics: Burnt Sienna, Napthol Crimson, Green Oxide, Burnt Umber
- Water-based varnish

Step-by-step painting of the Country Pear Tree Theorem.

Detail of pear tree.

Green, but the tips are Cadmium Yellow. Use Burnt Umber and Oxide of Chromium Green for the liner brush work.

FINISHING
THE THEOREM

Fill any gaps between the stencils using the liner brush and a drop of gum turps mixed with the appropriate colour. Use this method to paint in the veins of the leaves. Allow the theorem to dry for at least a week before framing.

STENCILLING
THE FRAME

Sand the pine frame and then brush on the shellac. Allow it to dry (approximately 30 minutes), lightly sand, then apply a second coat of shellac. Put the frame aside to dry.

Trace the frame design onto the acetate and cut out. Using the photograph as a guide, centre the prepared stencil onto the frame and tape in place.

Stencil all the houses around the frame with a mix of Burnt Sienna and Napthol Crimson. Mix a little Burnt Sienna with Green Oxide and stencil the trees, leaving the trees in the corners until last. Stencil all the trunks with Burnt Umber. Allow to dry.

With the soft brush, apply a coat of water-based varnish to the frame. Dry, then apply a second coat. When it is completely dry, frame the Country Pear Tree Theorem.

COUNTRY HOUSE THEOREM

PREPARATION

To prepare the painting surface and to cut the stencils, follow the instructions for the Country Pear Tree Theorem. The only difference is that four sheets of acetate will be needed for the Country House Theorem.

APPLYING THE COLOURS

Following the stencil diagrams provided on page 24, use Burnt Sienna for the house and chimney and Burnt Umber for the tree trunk, path, roof, fence rails and posts and windows. Mix the Burnt Umber and Alizarin Crimson oil paint for the door, and use Oxide of Chromium Green for the leaves and grass. The pears are a mix of Cadmium Yellow and Alizarin Crimson.

Use the liner brush and a drop of gum turps mixed with the appropriate colour, to fill any gaps between the stencils. Use this method to paint the window panes and the stems on the pears and leaves. Allow the theorem to dry for at least a week before framing.

COUNTRY HOUSE THEOREM

- 15cm x 20cm (6in x 8in) frame
- 15cm x 20cm (6in x 8in) white, acid-free cardboard
- 20cm x 25cm (8in x 10in) white cotton velveteen
- 4 sheets of A4 0.004 acetate film
- Archival Oil Paints: Burnt Umber, Burnt Sienna, Alizarin Crimson, Oxide of Chromium Green, Cadmium Yellow
- 1 extra-small stencil brush

Step-by-step painting of the Country House Theorem.

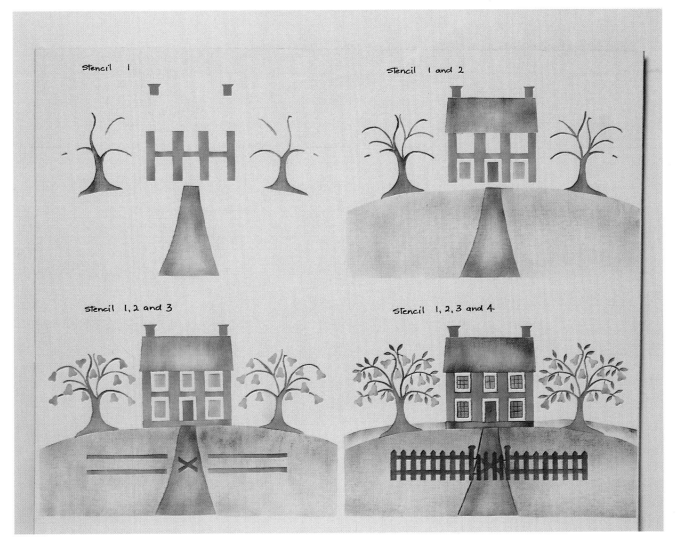

COUNTRY PEAR TREE THEOREM

Design Outline

COUNTRY HOUSE THEOREM

Design Outline

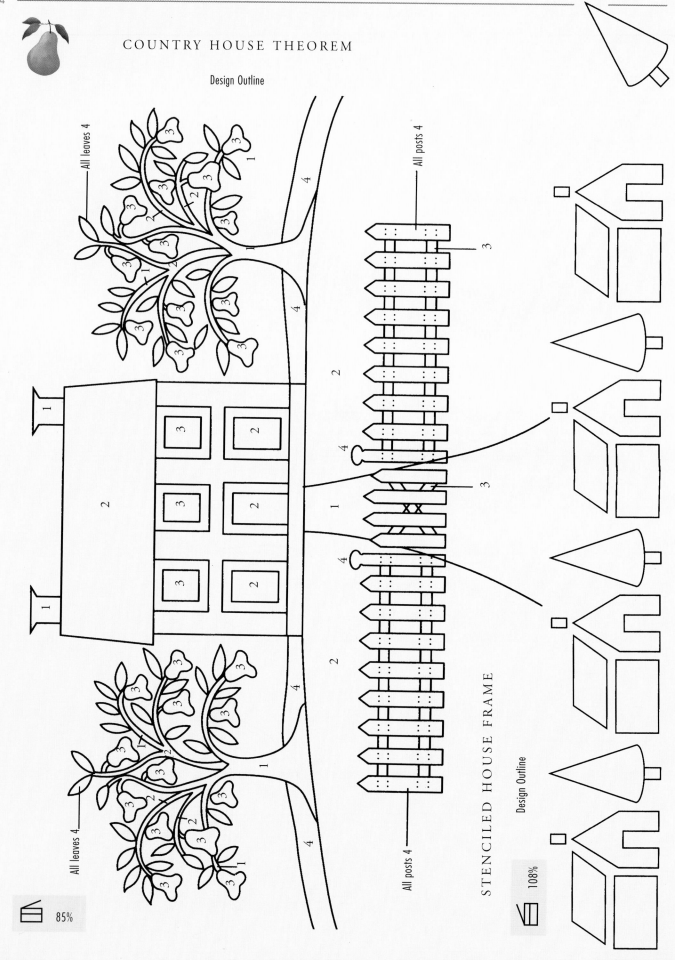

All leaves 4

All posts 4

STENCILED HOUSE FRAME

Design Outline

108%

85%

Fairy Quilt

Naive quilts use simple fabrics and shapes to achieve an innocent,
amusing effect which is perfect for a child's bedroom.
This quilt contains symbols and figures designed to awaken
a child's sense of wonder as well as encourage sweet dreams.

FINISHED SIZE

• 107cm x 79cm (42in x 31in)

MATERIALS

• Assorted fabrics for background, approximately three fat quarters

• Assorted scraps of fabric for appliqué shapes

• 30cm (⅓yd) fabric for sashings

• 45cm (½yd) fabric for border – 90cm (1yd) if the print has a directional pattern

• 60cm (⅔yd) fabric for bindings

• 90cm x 115cm (36in x 46in) backing fabric and batting

• Assorted buttons, beads and ribbon of your choice

• Thin cardboard for Appliqué method 1

• 45cm (½yd) Vliesofix for Appliqué method 2

• Rotary cutter, board and ruler

• Quilting cotton, Natural/Ecru and Dark Brown

• Masking tape for appliqué method 2

BEFORE YOU START

Study the pattern and read right through the instructions before you start this project, to make sure you have the necessary skills to complete it. You will find the pattern for this quilt on the Pattern Sheet.

Two methods of appliqué are used in this quilt. You can, if you prefer, use Appliqué Method 2 for all the pieces. It will only slightly alter the overall effect.

APPLIQUE METHOD 1

This is a traditional appliqué method in which a template of the shape is cut from thin cardboard. Tack the chosen fabric to the right side of the cardboard template, folding the raw edges over to the back of the cardboard. Press the edge-fold firmly, then remove the tacking and pin the shape into position on the background fabric. Attach the piece with a fine invisible appliqué stitch, using cotton to match the fabric of the piece.

APPLIQUE METHOD 2

This is a fast bonding method using Vliesofix. For this method all pieces must be traced from the reverse of the main pattern piece so that they will be facing the correct direction on your quilt. The easiest way to do this is to photocopy the pattern pieces that are to be appliquéd and to sticky tape the photocopy to the window, with the printed side facing the window. Use a pen to trace over the lines on the blank side of the photocopy. Cut out the pattern pieces and pin them, traced side up, on top of the Vliesofix. Cut out the Vliesofix to within 5mm (¼in) of the pen line and iron it onto the wrong side of your chosen fabric. Cut out on the pen line and peel the protective paper from the back. Place the shape onto the quilt and iron it into place. Stitch around the edge of each piece with buttonhole stitch using dark brown quilting cotton.

PIECING THE QUILT

Photocopy, or trace, the two halves of the master pattern on the Pattern Sheet and join the pieces together on a larger piece of paper. Lay out all background pieces as shown in the layout diagram. Cut sashing pieces 6.5cm (2½in) wide.

The seam allowance for all pieces is 5mm (¼in). Join the sections in Panels 1 and 3 and sew the sashing strips to the top and bottom of each panel as shown. Join panel 2 to panels 1 and 3 and sew on the side sashing strips.

BORDERS

From the border fabric cut three, 13cm (5in) strips. Cut one strip in half for the top and bottom border strips. The two long strips are for the side borders. Sew the top and bottom strips on first, then the two side borders. Press all seams towards the sashings. You are now ready to appliqué your shapes onto the completed background.

APPLIQUEING
THE DESIGN

First select your fabrics for each shape. It is a good idea to tape small snippets of fabric to the master pattern to help with your colour selections. Trace the shapes onto cardboard or Vliesofix, depending on the method indicated in Appliqué method 1 and 2. Remember to reverse the pattern pieces for method 2.

To add further interest to your quilt, some of the hearts and the moon can be pieced and then cut out, then tacked to cardboard templates.

QUILTING

❖

Iron the backing fabric for the quilt and place it face down on a table. Place the batting on top of the backing and then the completed quilt top, facing up. Baste the three layers together securely. Quilt around each shape outline with natural quilting thread. Add buttons, ribbon, beads and any other embellishments.

BINDING

❖

Cut four lengths, 115cm x 15cm (1¼ yds x 6in) from the binding fabric. With wrong sides together, fold the strips in half and press. Attach the side bindings first. With right sides facing, machine-stitch the binding around the front edges of the quilt. Trim away any excess batting and backing to 2.5cm (1in) from the stitching line. Turn the binding to the back of the quilt and firmly slip stitch it in place.

Repeat on the top and bottom of the quilt, but add an extra 2.5cm (1in) to the ends of these binding strips. Turn the ends under and stitch to neaten the corners.

HANGING HEARTS

❖

For each of the five hearts cut two, 12cm (4⅝in) squares of fabric and one square of batting. Place the two fabric squares right sides together with the batting square on the bottom. Trace the heart pattern onto the top wrong side of the fabric square. Machine-stitch around the edge and trim the excess away. Make a 2.5cm (1in) slit in the middle of the top layer of fabric and turn the heart right side out, through the slit.

Cut five strips of fabric 15cm x 20cm (6in x 8in) long. Fold each strip in half widthways, then in half again to give a finished width of 3.7cm (1½in). Machine-stitch down each side to neaten. Fold the finished strip in half and place behind the heart, leaving enough room in the loop for the hanging rod.

Place the five hearts across the top of the quilt, measuring an equal distance between them. Stitch the hearts to the quilt. Add a button to the centre of each heart for decoration and to secure the hanging tab.

Layout diagram for the background pieces.

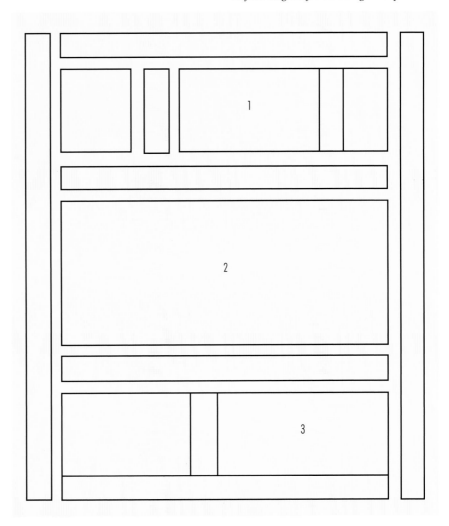

Country Mouse

It is hard to believe this charming creature is made from
such simple materials as flour, salt and water. Salt dough can be used
to model figures in a similar way to modelling clay, without the need
of a kiln — simply pop your models in the oven.

FINISHED SIZE

- Approximately 20cm (8in)

MATERIALS

For one batch of dough:

- 2 cups of plain flour
- ½ cup salt
- 1 cup of hot tap water
- 1 teaspoon glycerine
- 1 teaspoon food colouring or acrylic paint, brown and green

Other requirements:

- Aluminium foil
- Rolling pin
- 2 peppercorns
- Bristles for whiskers
- Knife for cutting dough
- Modelling tools
- Scissors
- Clear gloss polyurethane varnish, not water-based
- Fine felt-tip black pen
- White acrylic paint
- Fine brush or stylus
- 25cm (10in) square pine frame
- Craft glue
- Small heart-shaped cutter
- Dried flowers and Spanish moss
- Raffia for bow
- Toothpick

PREPARING THE DOUGH

You will need to make three batches of the dough mix. Leave one uncoloured, make one green and one brown.

For each batch, mix the flour and salt together. If colouring the dough, add one teaspoon of food colouring or acrylic paint to the cup of hot tap water and stir. Add the water and colour to the flour and salt. Knead the mixture well for a few minutes. The dough is ready when it is smooth and pliable. Keep each of the batches in cling wrap or a plastic bag so they do not dry out.

Cut a piece of foil to place your mouse on as you assemble the pieces and keep a bowl of water nearby to moisten the edges of each piece as you join them together.

MOULDING THE LEGS

Roll a cylinder of uncoloured dough 8cm long by 1cm thick (3¼in x ½in). Cut this in half and form together in a V shape.

For the shoes, roll a marble-sized ball of green dough into an oval shape. Moisten the edges of the legs with water, and attach the shoes. Use a toothpick to make the shoelace holes.

MAKING THE GARMENTS

Using a rolling pin, roll out a piece of brown dough until it is approximately 3mm–4mm (⅛in) thick. Using the pattern provided, cut out the underskirt. Centre the underskirt across the legs leaving the shoes showing. Gently mould

the dough into the desired shape, gathering and pinching as required.

Repeat these steps for the dress using brown dough. Attach over the underskirt, leaving about 2cm (¾in) of the underskirt showing. Make the apron from uncoloured dough and attach it on top of the dress.

ATTACHING THE ARMS

Using green dough, roll out a 15cm (6in) long cylinder and attach this to the top of the body, so the ends form the arms. Mould small pieces of uncoloured dough into oval shapes for the paws. Use a toothpick to mark the paws.

Once the arms are in place, the collar can be positioned so that it covers the top of the arms. Roll out a piece of uncoloured dough and use the pattern to cut out the collar shape. Crimp the edges of the collar to form a frilly edge.

MOULDING THE HEAD

Mould a walnut-sized piece of uncoloured dough into the shape of a mouse's head. Attach this to the neck on top of the collar, moistening the pieces with water. Place two peppercorns about halfway down the face for the eyes and use a moulding tool to shape the mouth. Stick in the bristles to represent whiskers and trim them to the desired length. Roll a small ball of dough and press with your finger to mould each ear and attach to the head.

Roll out a rectangle of green dough 12cm x 1cm (4¾in x ⅞in) for the bow. Form the rectangle into two loops and pinch the ends and the centre together. Attach the bow between the ears.

1. *Assemble the mouse on a piece of foil. Begin with the legs and shoes, then add the clothes in layers.*

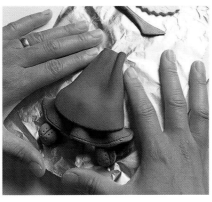

2. *As each garment piece is added, mould into the required shape.*

3. *Once the main garment pieces are in place, the head and smaller details can be added.*

FINISHING TOUCHES

Using a small heart-shaped cutter, cut out one heart from the brown dough and one from the green and attach them to the apron using the photograph as a guide. Cut small circles of uncoloured dough to make the buttons, and mark the buttonholes with a toothpick. The tail is a thin coil 9cm (3½in) long made from uncoloured dough and is attached on the right side of the dress.

Mould the baby mouse from uncoloured dough using the photograph as a guide, and attach it to the mother's arms.

Make the baby as shown and attach it to the mother's arms, then bake. After baking, add the final details with a fine, felt-tip pen or acrylic paint.

BAKING THE DOUGH

Place the mice on an oven tray and bake them at a low temperature (100–125 degrees Celsius or 210–250 degrees Fahrenheit) until the dough is completely hard. Test for hardness by pressing in at the thickest part. If there is any give at all, continue baking.

When completely cool, use acrylic paints and a fine brush, or a felt-tip pen, to add any extra details such as dots, stitching lines and bows.

Seal with at least two coats of polyurethane varnish to preserve and protect the figures. Allow at least two days for the varnish to dry.

ASSEMBLY

Glue the mouse into the pine frame using a good craft glue. Glue in the dried flowers and Spanish moss around the figure as desired. Tie a raffia bow and glue it to the edge of the frame.

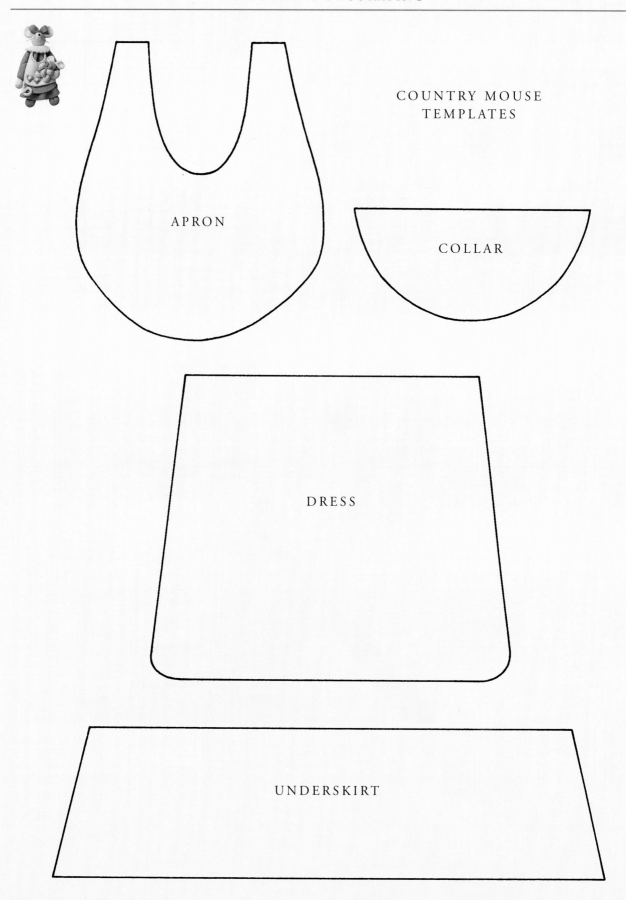

COUNTRY MOUSE
TEMPLATES

APRON

COLLAR

DRESS

UNDERSKIRT

 SS

Pumpkin Harvest

This striking, naive-style appliqué captures the rich colours of the harvest.
Stitched on an even-weave, unbleached linen background, it is quick
and easy to complete and is ideal for a first attempt at appliqué.
The rustic design will look right at home in a country kitchen.

FINISHED SIZE

- 30cm x 22 cm (12in x 9in) (excluding frame)

MATERIALS

- 45cm x 35cm (18in x 14in) piece of even-weave, unbleached linen
- Scraps of 100 per cent cotton fabric for pumpkins and stalks
- White paper for tracing patterns
- Two shades of brown sewing thread
- Greaseproof or tracing paper
- Felt-tip pen
- Tracing paper
- General sewing requirements

1. *Cut shapes from fabric adding a 3–4mm seam allowance.*

2. *Baste the shapes to the paper templates and press.*

3. *Remove the paper, and press the shapes again.*

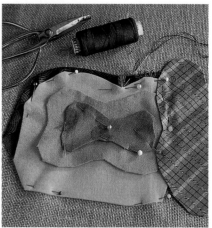

4. *Pin overlapping pieces in place before stitching.*

PREPARATION

Using the felt-tip pen trace or photocopy the pattern onto white paper, then trace each individual shape onto tracing paper. Where shapes overlap with other shapes on the pattern, draw the lines where you assume they would be. Cut out the individual pieces.

Pin the pattern pieces onto the desired fabric scraps and cut around each piece, adding a 3–4mm (⅜in) seam allowance around the outside edge of all pieces (see Step 1). Fold all raw edges to the wrong side and, using small basting

stitches, sew the fabric to the paper, clipping curves as you go where required. Press the folds with a steam iron (see Step 2). Just before you are ready to stitch each shape in place, remove the basting and paper and press the piece again (see Step 3).

For the skin of the pumpkin, cut a strip of fabric approximately 30cm x 2.5cm (12in x 1in). Fold the fabric in half with wrong sides together and raw edges even. Press the fold firmly.

APPLIQUE METHOD

Centre the design on the linen and pin each shape into position, making

sure that those that are overlapped are pinned in place first (see Step 4). Thread the needle with a double thread of the lighter brown colour and, following the photograph, attach the interior pieces of the Queensland Blue pumpkin using large basting stitches and random, large cross stitches.

Attach the outside of each pumpkin with straight stitch using a double thread of the darker brown colour. Use a single thread of the lighter colour to back stitch the lines on the orange pumpkins.

When all the stitching is complete, give your piece a final press and frame your work as desired.

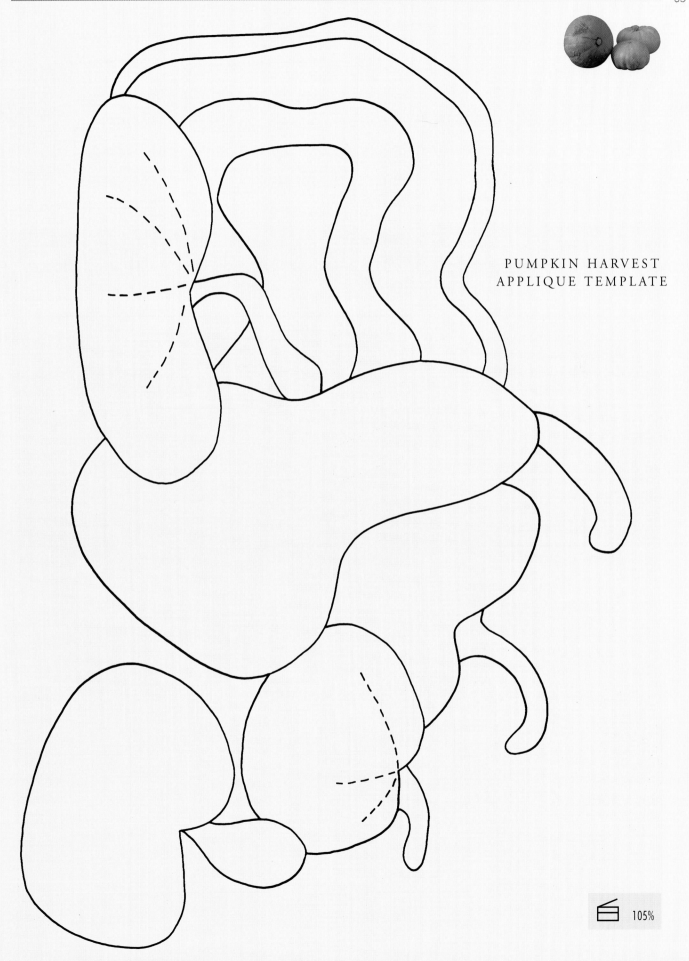

PUMPKIN HARVEST
APPLIQUE TEMPLATE

105%

Blue Braids

Born out of necessity in pioneer days when every scrap of fabric was precious, braided rugs are easy and inexpensive to make — particularly if you use scrap fabrics. This simple project can be made as colourful and as large as you like.

CHOOSING FABRICS

There are no right or wrong ways to choose the fabrics for your rug and the choice depends on the effect you wish to achieve. The following guidelines will help with your colour choices.

A predominance of prints will give you a country look, while using more plain fabrics will give your rug a contemporary feel.

If you wish to achieve an effect similar to the rug featured in this project, work with one colour family at a time, choosing three to five fabrics in the same family, that range from light to dark. Choose a variety of textures, plains, prints and stripes. For our rug, we used fabrics from three colour families. We chose plain beige, beige check, beige floral, plain dark forest green, green check, multi-coloured floral, plain purple, plain light purple and purple floral.

A different effect is achieved if you combine colours from two different families. Choose light, medium and dark of each colour and vary the patterns of the fabrics. You can achieve a tweedy look by combining colours that have a sharp contrast, such as beige, green and purple.

If you should run out of a colour while plaiting, replace it with a similar fabric of the same colour tone so that the change will not be obvious.

PREPARING FABRIC STRIPS

Cut or tear fabrics into 10cm (4in) wide strips approximately 2m (2yds) in length, joining strips if necessary. Fold the edges of the strip to the wrong side almost to the centre, then fold it in half. The strip will now be approximately one quarter its original width, and the raw edges will be concealed. Roll the strips up and secure with elastic bands.

THE PLAIT

Select three strips for the centre of the rug. Open out two of the strips leaving the raw edges tucked under, and stitch them together on the bias. Trim the corner away and fold the strip down the centre again. Place the third strip at the join to form a T, then stitch along the bottom edge of the joined strips where the three strips meet (see photograph below). Fold the top of the T over and hold the three strips with the bulldog clip (see photograph next page). Secure it to a hook, (the cotton reel holder on your sewing machine is ideal) to give you tension for plaiting. Plait the strip, pulling gently as you go.

FINISHED SIZE

- 80cm x 52cm (31/2in x 201/2in)

MATERIALS

- 11m (111/2yds) of nine different 100 per cent cotton fabrics
- 30m (32yds) linen thread
- Curved sewing needle
- Medium-size bulldog clip
- Elastic bands
- Safety pin
- General sewing requirements

Join two strips on the bias and then stitch the third strip in place to form a T.

Hold the joined edges of the three strips with a bulldog clip.

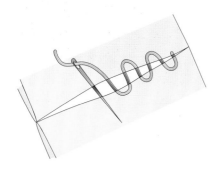

To form the oval, join the braid together using ladder stitch.

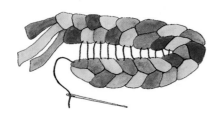

THE OVAL

Complete approximately 30cm (12in) of plaiting (or whatever length you have planned) and attach a safety pin to mark the point. It is this first braid that determines the shape of your oval — the longer the centre braid the more elongated the shape), so you need to make this decision now. Work another 40cm (16in) of braid, then bend the braid at the safety pin. Using the linen thread and ladder stitch, sew each inside loop of the two braids together (see diagrams left). When you come to your first bend, ease the braid around the curve. The curve will grow as each row of braid is added. Put your needle through two loops on the top braid and one loop on the bottom braid. The aim is to make the coils lay flat.

A NEW STRIP

When you want to join a new strip, join them together on the bias in the same way as the first two strips were joined. When working an oval rug, change colours when the centre is complete.

To ensure that you have the same number of rows on each side of the centre braid you must always change strips on the left side of the first bend of the centre braid.

To keep the colours flowing smoothly and to prevent them looking 'chopped off', only make colour changes one strip at a time. Braid the new strip in with two of the old stips and work a whole round with this new combination, before braiding in a second strip of another new colour.

ENDING THE RUG

When your rug is the size you desire, stitch it to within 20cm (8in) of the finishing point. The finishing point should be in line with your colour change point.

Braid 4cm (1½in) past where you will end. Cut the ends of the braid, then unbraid the plait and cut the three strips off at different points. Taper the strips by cutting away some of the fullness of the fabric. To prevent the strips from fraying, turn the bottom raw edges in and hand stitch the sides and bottom edges together.

Braid these strips as much as you can then sew the shortest strip under one of the other two. Twist the two remaining strips around each other and then sew them together.

The rug may have pulled out of shape as you have been working. If so, lay it on a flat surface, push and pull it into shape and press with a damp cloth.

Home-made Happiness

Though developed for novice sewers to practise their stitches, the sampler remains popular with cross-stitchers of all aptitudes. This sampler is an interesting challenge for experienced cross-stitchers, or it can be made simpler by working only the top section or individual motifs.

FINISHED SIZE

• 33cm x 22½cm (13in x 9in) (excluding frame)

MATERIALS

• 54cm x 50cm (22in x 20in) cream Aida cloth (16 threads per inch)

• DMC Stranded Embroidery Cotton: one each of 947 (Burnt Orange), 839 (Beige Brown), 321 (Christmas Red), 797 (Royal Blue), 798 (Dk Delft), 799 (Med. Delft), 906 (Parrot Green), 444 (Dk Lemon), 919 (Red Copper), 470 (Lt Avocado Green), 937 (Med. Avocado Green), 3731 (V. Dk Dusty Rose), 727 (V. Lt Topaz), 310 (Black), 353 (Peach Flesh), 3041 (Antique Violet), 422 (Lt Hazel Nut Brown), 522 (Fern Green), 520 (Dk Fern Green), 926 (Med. Grey Green), 3768 (Dk Grey Green), 924 (V. Dk Grey Green), 340 (Blue Violet), 826 (Med. Blue), 726 (Topaz), 733 (Med. Olive Green), 347 (V. Dk Salmon), 730 (V. Dk Olive Green), 761 (Lt Salmon), 760 (Salmon), 971 (Pumpkin), 831 (Med. Golden Olive), 552 (Med. Violet), 554 (Lt Violet), 922 (Lt Copper), 648 (Lt Beaver Grey), 747 (V. Lt Sky Blue), 815 (Med. Garnet), 469 (Avocado Green), 720 (Dk Orange Spice), 327 (V. Dk Violet), 809 (Delft), 791 (V. Dk Cornflower Blue), 902 (V. Dk Garnet), 318 (Lt Steel Grey), 729 (Med. Old Gold), 420 (Dk Hazel Nut Brown), 702 (Kelly Green), 700 (Bright Christmas Green), 3347 (Med. Yellow Green), 523 (Lt Fern Green), 632 (Med. Negro Flesh), 796 (Dk Royal Blue), 3371 (Black Brown), and White (Blanc)

• Size 26 tapestry needle

• Embroidery scissors

PREPARATION

Overlock or zigzag stitch around the edge of the Aida cloth to prevent fraying. Fold the fabric in half and then into quarters. Baste vertically and horizontally along these folds through the centre point.

So that it is easier to work from, enlarge the stitch guide on a photocopier. If you wish, you can also colour the grid and the colour key to help distinguish the symbols. Also rule vertical and horizontal lines through the centre of the graph to match the basting guides on the cloth. Following the grid of the graph as a guide, baste around the edge of the sampler area, marking it into quarters.

CROSS-STITCH

Using the colours indicated in the key, work all the cross-stitches in two strands of embroidery thread. Except for the background, which is left unembroidered, areas that have been left blank such as the dolls' aprons, jam jar labels and the cloth in the embroidery hoop, are embroidered in white. Do not knot your thread; instead, secure it by holding an inch of thread behind the cloth and cross stitching over it to hold it in place.

BACK STITCH

When you have finished the cross-stitching, back stitch the letters and the following outlines using one thread of the appropriate stranded cotton. Use 3371 (Black Brown) for all the letters and numbers; 310 (Black) for the dolls' aprons, embroidery in the hoop, needles, jam jars and labels; and 422 (Lt Hazel Nut) for the wooden cotton reels. The long straight lines of letters such as 'W' and 'Z' can be worked by laying one long stitch from point to point, then couching it down with tiny stitches.

Back stitch the following outlines using two threads of stranded cotton:

470 (Lt Avocado Green) for the cotton in the embroidery; 522 (Fern Green) for the cotton on the upper reel; 3347 (Med. Yellow Green) for the cotton on the lower reel; and 919 (Red Copper) around the flower pot.

FINISHING

Once all the embroidery has been completed, remove the basting threads and gently wash the fabric using warm water and pure soap. Rinse thoroughly. Do not squeeze or wring out, but roll in a towel to remove excess water and lay flat on the open towel to dry. Press with a moderately hot iron. The piece is now ready to be framed.

KEY TO DMC STRANDED COTTONS

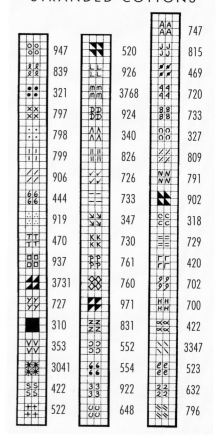

		747
947	520	815
839	926	469
321	3768	720
797	924	733
798	340	327
799	826	809
906	726	791
444	733	902
919	347	318
470	730	729
937	761	420
3731	760	702
727	971	700
310	831	422
353	552	3347
3041	554	523
422	922	632
522	648	796

After you have photocopied the two pattern pieces on this page and the following page, match them up by aligning line A of the first half with line A of the second half. This will give you the complete pattern.

Cottage Garden

Capture the charm of a cottage garden on a terracotta pot.
Although created for a circular pot, the pattern could be adapted
to suit different shapes. The design is best applied with a free brush style,
and some prior experience of folk art painting is recommended.

FINISHED SIZE

- 15cm x 30.5cm (6in x 12in) (design only)

MATERIALS

- 21½cm (8½in) diameter terracotta pot
- Sponge (synthetic or sea)
- Acrylic sealer or Bondcrete
- 5mm (¼in) tape
- Tracing paper (if required)
- Chalk pencil
- 25mm (1in) large flat brush
- No 3 round brush
- No 5 round brush
- No 0 liner brush
- Fan brush (optional)
- Stencil brush (optional)
- Jo Sonja's Artists' Acrylics: Pine Green, Mars Black, Jade, Red Earth, Gold Oxide, Turners Yellow, Warm White, Titanium White, Napthol Red Light, Yellow Oxide, Burgundy, Raw Sienna, Norwegian Orange, Yellow Light, Hookers Green, Antique Green, Moss Green, Teal Green, Green Oxide, Ultramarine, Sapphire.

Sponge the outside surface with a mix of Hookers Green and Mars Black.

PREPARATION

❖

Seal the terracotta pot inside and out, using the large brush and acrylic sealer. Allow the sealer to dry, then sponge the entire outside surface with a mixture of equal parts Black and Hookers Green.

Press strips of 5mm (¼in) tape onto the outside of the pot approximately 1.5cm (⅝in) apart. With the chalk pencil, mark a line between the tapes approximately two thirds of the way up the pot. This is the top of the pickets. Heavily load the No 5 round brush with Warm White. Flair the brush carefully to create the rounded top of each picket and paint each space between the tape strips, covering the green completely with Warm White. Allow the paint to dry completely then remove the tape by pulling down from the top, keeping the tape as close to the painting as possible.

After painting the pickets, remove the tape by pulling down from the top.

Sponge an uneven line approximately half to two thirds of the way up the pickets.

Sponge an uneven line half to two thirds of the way up the pickets, with a mix of Teal Green, Green Oxide and Pine Green. Turn the sponge between dabs to make the colours interesting and not repetitive. Allow the paint to dry.

At this stage you can, if you wish, apply the pattern of the hollyhocks randomly around the piece to act as a positional.

Add more white to the warm gold mix and dab irregular rows of ovals from the top to the bottom of the tall triangle, with the smallest at the top and the largest at the base. Change to a watery Raw Sienna and dab small circles at the base of each of the ovals. This colour must be transparent. With the liner brush, paint leaves at the tip of the triangle.

ANEMONES

These are just filler flowers for any gaps around the daisy bushes. Load the No 3 round with Norwegian Orange and a side-load of Yellow Light and paint three small comma strokes next to each other and joining at the base. Paint a stem with a mix of Pine Green and Turners Yellow.

HOLLYHOCKS

With Jade on the liner brush draw in the stems of the hollyhocks, some slightly crooked, and either stroke the leaves with a side load of Pine Green now, or after you've painted the flowers.

Mix Warm White with a touch of Burgundy, Red Earth and Yellow Oxide to make warm pink. With the No 3 round brush paint the flowers in an amoeba shape, getting smaller towards the top of the stem. Make some side facing flowers by painting rounded triangles.

Add more Warm White to the pink mix and with the liner brush, draw double thin wavy lines around the outer edge of each flower. For the side facing flowers, cut the lines across the triangles from corner to corner and around the bottom side. Mix a dark pink with Burgundy, Red Earth and a little Warm White and crisscross some fine lines in the centre of each flower.

LAVENDER

Make a silvery green by mixing Antique Green, Warm White and a touch of Mars Black and with the liner brush, paint an upside-down umbrella shape for the stems of the lavender. Turn the pot upside down to help make the stems thinner and longer. Place them between and over the hollyhocks and foxgloves.

On the brush mix a varied mauve-purple from Burgundy, Ultramarine, Sapphire and Warm White. Point the bristles of the brush sideways and dab diminishing rows of blobs up each stem in purples and an occasional side-load of Warm White.

FORGET-ME-NOTS

Use either a double loaded fan brush or a No 3 round kept flattened and spiky-loaded with Ultramarine and Titanium White. After dabbing the blue and white around the base of the daisy bushes, dot in some blue mini-flowers here and there with the liner brush. Finish with a centre dot of Turners Yellow.

FINISHING

Apply a brick-paved pathway around the pot to finish the design. Base in a stripe of Gold Oxide below the forget-me-nots, then paint the bricks over the top in Red Earth. If this path cuts off the green rather abruptly, go back and dry brush or scumble some Green Oxide and Pine Green over the edge of the path.

DAISY BUSHES

Sponge or stumble with a stencil brush, an uneven row of bushes over the bases of the previous flowers using a various mix of Moss Green, Green Oxide and Antique Green. When this is completely dry, use the tip of the No 3 round to stroke in the daisies with Titanium White. The centres are a push-dab stroke using Napthol Red Light with a side-load of Yellow Light. If the areas between the daisies seem a bit bland, use a liner brush to stroke in some stems and side leaves.

FOXGLOVES

Mix a warm gold with Warm White, Gold Oxide and Turners Yellow. With a No 3 round brush, base in a tall triangle for each Foxglove stem around the pot between the hollyhocks, in pairs or singles. Add a stem in Green Oxide and Warm White.

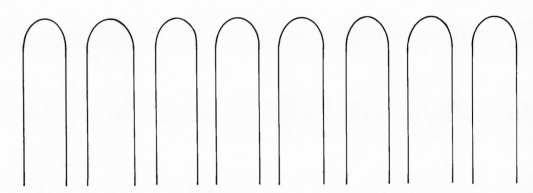

COTTAGE GARDEN

Design outlines

Scatter hollyhocks first.

Picket fence on top of base.

Sponging — sponge again
after the tape is removed.

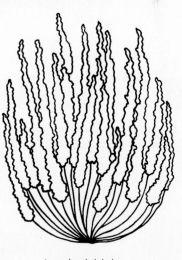

Foxgloves between
hollyhocks.

Lavender slightly lower
than first flowers.

Sponge lighter green bushes over stems of
the flowers below then dab daisies all over.

Anenomes, between daisy bushes.

Forget-me-nots at the base of green.

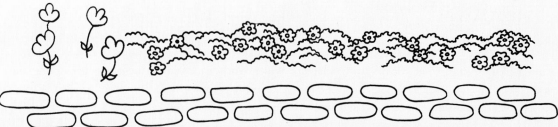

Bricks (optional).

 127%

Tea for Two

*Add country style to your breakfast table with this simple-to-make
tea-cosy. The pattern can easily be enlarged to fit any teapot.
This is an ideal gift for a tea-drinking friend, so make one for
your favourite teapot and one to give away.*

FINISHED SIZE

- 45cm x 17cm (17¾in x 6¾in) — made to fit small to medium teapot

MATERIALS

- 50cm x 20cm (20in x 8in) large-check fabric remnant
- 50cm x 20cm (20in x 8in) floral fabric remnant
- 50cm x 20cm (20in x 8in) thin craft batting
- Matching thread
- 1m (1⅛yd) ribbon
- 2 flower-shaped buttons (or 10 small shirt buttons)
- Green embroidery thread
- Tracing or grease-proof paper
- Sticky tape
- Fine permanent pen, Artline Drawing System 0.2 or similar
- General sewing requirements

PREPARATION

This cover is designed to fit a small to medium teapot, so enlarge the rectangular pattern piece if you are making a cover for a larger teapot.

Cut three rectangular pieces from the pattern — one piece from the check fabric, one from the floral and one from the batting. On the check fabric, align the dashed squares on the pattern with a white check. Arrange the pattern piece on the floral fabric so the design is regular.

Trace the words 'Tea for Two' from the pattern on page 49 onto tracing or greaseproof paper and then sticky tape the tracing paper onto a window. Position the fabric over this and transfer the design using the permanent pen. Turn the fabric around and repeat for the other end. Make sure your 'Tea for Two' faces the right way when you have finished the cosy. Position the flower buttons and stitch them in place using three strands of green embroidery thread. Continue with this thread to complete the stem of the flower using back stitch and lazy daisy stitch.

If you are unable to find suitable flower buttons, use five small, odd shirt buttons for each flower. The buttons do not need to be exactly the same size or colour, in fact, it will look better if they are varied.

CONSTRUCTION

With right side facing upward, place the front of the cosy on top of the batting and pin in place around the edge. Cut the ribbon into four equal pieces, fold over one end of each piece and machine-stitch the ribbons to the cosy in the positions indicated on the pattern. Place the inside fabric piece on top of the front side, right sides facing. Pin the three layers together. Machine-stitch around the outside edges leaving a 10cm (4in) opening for turning. Clip the corners at least 3mm (⅛in) from the stitching and turn the fabric through to the right side. Roll the seams to the edge and press. Stitch around the outside edge of the cosy to create a neat edge and to close the opening.

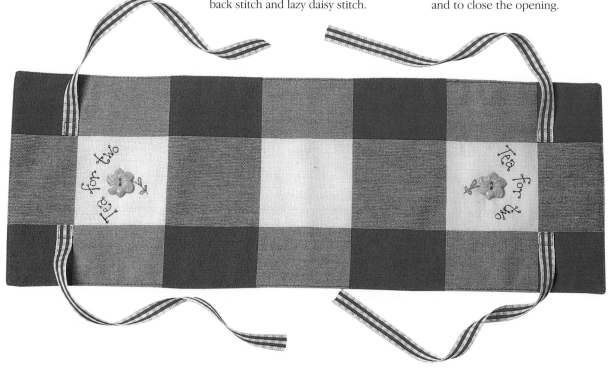

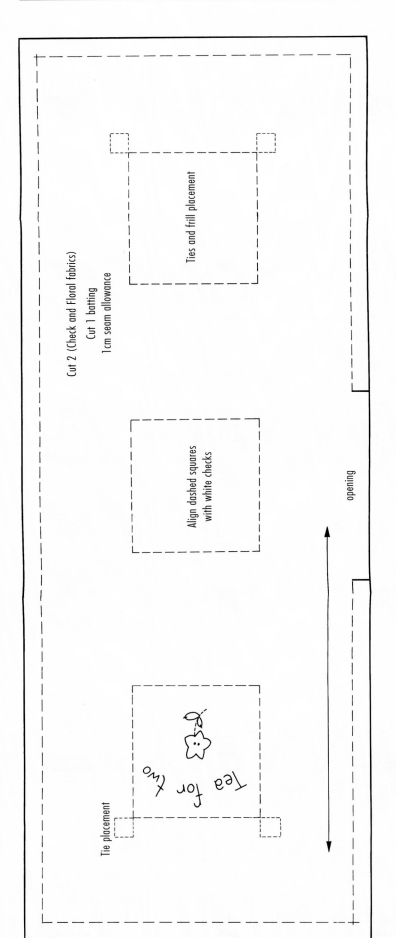

Cut 2 (Check and Floral fabrics)
Cut 1 batting
1cm seam allowance

Ties and frill placement

Align dashed squares
with white checks

Tie placement

Tea for two

opening

TEA FOR TWO
TEA-COSY

Pattern

TEA-COSY
Construction Diagram

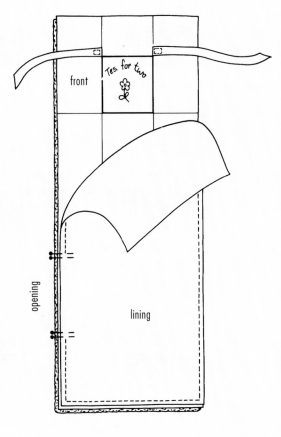

front

Tea for two

opening

lining

200%

Restored Treasures

Most of us are reluctant to throw away items we no longer use
if we can see a way to recycle them. The following projects demonstrate
how new life can be given to a range of pre-used objects, and how
attractive items for the home can be made from nature's bounty.

Sunflower Surprise

The beauty of the harvest is reflected in this country-style floral arrangement. Flowers, twigs and leaves have been chosen to complement the colours and textures of the pumpkin. Use the removed pulp for pumpkin soup and nothing of this attractive vegetable is wasted.

PREPARATION

Soak the oasis in water for at least an hour beforehand. Sit the pumpkin on a flat surface and decide where the hole is to be cut. It may be off-centre if the base of the pumpkin does not sit flat. Using a kitchen knife, cut a hole about 10cm (4in) in diameter in the top of the pumpkin. Take care not to cut the hole too large, as the flowers need to be grouped close together for the best effect.

Scoop out all the centre pulp and seeds, then clean away any loose strands of fibre. Trim the oasis to fit snugly into the hole in the pumpkin, leaving about 2cm (¾in) raised above the top to allow for easy insertion of the flowers.

ARRANGING THE FLOWERS

The charm of this design is in its compact and integrated shape, achieved by keeping the colour contrasts in close relationship with each other.

Cut the stems of the three sunflowers to lengths of about 12cm, 14cm and 15cm (5in, 5½in and 6in) and push them into the oasis, keeping them close to each other. These are the focal point of the arrangement, so ensure they are securely fixed into the oasis before you add the other flowers.

Cut one twisted twig or tortured willow to a length of about 50cm (20in) and push it into the oasis behind the sunflowers to provide interesting height to the arrangement. Place the second twig behind the sunflowers at a contrasting angle to the first.

Cut each of the leucadendron heads to a length of about 15cm (6in) from the tip of the petals to the end of the stem and insert them to the left of the sunflowers,

arranging them in a close group.

The daisy chrysanthemums, which have several blooms on a stalk, should be cut to between 10cm and 15cm (4in–6in), grouped together and inserted behind and to the right of the sunflowers.

Cut the statice to about 15cm (6in) lengths and insert between the groups of colour and under the front of the sunflowers to add colour highlights.

FINISHING

The final details will provide a professional touch to your arrangement. To place the stalks of wheat, follow the line of the twisted twig in the centre and keep the height midway between the top of the twig and the sunflowers. Insert stalks of baby's breath in any gaps to create a soft, light effect.

The finishing touch is to add the spear grass loops. Cut them to three different lengths. Those in the photograph are 10cm, 35cm and 65cm (4in, 14in and

MATERIALS

- Large pumpkin (the one in the photograph is approximately 70cm [27⅝in] in diameter)
- Block of green oasis, approximately 10cm (4in) square
- Sharp kitchen knife

Any flowers may be used. The ones in the arrangement illustrated are:

- 3 sunflowers
- 5 stems of leucadendrons
- 10–15 red daisy chrysanthemums
- 2 stems of twisted twig or tortured willow
- 3 stems of coloured statice
- Stems of baby's breath
- 8–10 stalks of wheat
- 3 stalks of spear grass

25¾in). Group them at the back of the arrangement, with both ends inserted into the oasis to create a looped effect.

Place your country flowers on a low table to enjoy the contrasts of colour, shape and texture. Add water occasionally to freshen the flowers.

Wildberry Canisters

Create your own attractive storage containers from empty food tins with resealable lids. Choose a background colour to suit your kitchen decor, or use the colours recommended below. This is a perfect project for anyone new to folk art techniques.

PREPARATION

Lightly scuff the surface of the tins to remove the shine. This can be done with fine wet-and-dry sandpaper, fine steel wool or with a scouring pad and detergent. Rinse thoroughly and allow to dry.

With a basecoating brush, apply sealer in criss-cross brush strokes over a small area, brushing back and forth several times until the sealer is almost dry. Then move on to another section and repeat until the entire surface is covered. Allow to dry thoroughly. Apply three coats of Antique White and leave to dry.

TRANSFERRING THE DESIGN

Trace the No 1 design from page 57 onto tracing paper. Place the tracing paper on the can in the desired position and secure it with magic tape. Slip a sheet of grey transfer paper between the surface of the can and the tracing, and transfer the pattern with a stylus or ballpoint pen. Use the No 10 flat brush to apply two coats of Ebony Black over the traced area and allow to dry.

Trace and then apply the No 2 design on page 57 over the black outline, using the white transfer paper.

PAINTING THE DESIGN

LEAVES

Load the No 4 flat brush with Forest Green and paint the leaves marked as '1' on the pattern near the No 2 design. Load the liner brush with a mix of Reindeer Moss Green and Forest Green and paint the stems. Still using the flat brush, paint the leaves marked '2' with Reindeer Moss Green. Use the liner brush for the stems. For the remaining small leaves and stems use a mix of Reindeer Moss Green and Berry Red on the round brush.

RASPBERRIES

On your palette place chocolate-chip sized puddles of Berry Red and Lavender, ensuring they are just touching. Dip a cotton bud into the centre of the two colours. The cotton bud should have Berry Red on one side and Lavender on the other. Touch the bud to the surface of the palette a couple of times to remove excess paint and then place five dots side by side as shown in the Painting Guide on page 56. Reload the cotton bud as necessary and use a new bud when it starts to lose its shape. Allow the paint to dry and repeat if necessary. Load a liner brush with Light Buttermilk and paint a tiny comma on one side of each dot for the highlight.

BLUEBERRIES

Place puddles of Country Blue and Primary Blue on your palette as described in the raspberry instructions. Dip a cotton bud to pick up Country Blue on one side and Primary Blue, on the other and place the dots as demonstrated in the painting instructions. Allow the paint to dry and repeat if necessary.

Load the liner brush with Light Buttermilk and paint a tiny comma on one side of each berry for the highlight. Reload the same brush with thinned Ebony Black and paint in the stems and blossom ends.

DAISIES

Form the daisies by dipping the handle end of a brush into Light Buttermilk and adding four even dots as shown in the Painting Guide. Add a dot of Berry Red to the centre of the flower.

MATERIALS

- Recycled food tins with lids — at least 10cm (4in) in diameter and 12cm (4¾in) tall
- Fine wet-and-dry sandpaper or fine steel wool
- Jo Sonja's All Purpose Sealer
- Tracing paper
- Grey and white transfer paper
- Stylus or ballpoint pen
- Magic tape
- 20mm (¾in) basecoating brush
- No 4 flat brush
- Liner brush
- No 2 round brush
- No 10 flat brush
- Cotton buds
- Old toothbrush
- DecoArt Americana Acrylics: Antique White, Ebony Black, Forest Green, Reindeer Moss Green, Berry Red, Lavender, Light Buttermilk, Country Blue, Primary Blue, Moon Yellow
- Satin finish varnish

LETTERING

Load a liner brush with Moon Yellow, thinned with a little water, and paint in the letters. It may be necessary to paint on the letters with two coats. Dip the handle end of the brush into the paint and place a dot on the joins of each letter.

FINISHING

Protect surrounding areas with newspaper. Mix together whatever is left on the palette to make a dark brown colour and thin to a milky consistency. Dip a toothbrush into a mixture, point the bristles of the toothbrush towards the painted surface and run your thumb over the bristles to produce specks of paint. Practise on the newspaper first before spattering the tins.

Allow the canisters to dry thoroughly before finishing with approximately three coats of satin varnish.

Painting Guide

**WILDBERRY
CANISTERS**
Design Outline

No 1

Milo Tea Coffee

No 2

Sugar

Pinwheel and Star Quilt

*The best quilts are those with memories attached. This quilt was made
from scraps given to the designer by friends when she was returning
home from America. It was hand-pieced and hand-quilted
on the journey and while she waited for her possessions to arrive.*

PREPARATION

Using template plastic, trace Templates for A, B, C and D from the full-size Block Diagram on page 62 and E from the Corner Block Diagram on page 61, then cut them out.

CUTTING

Cut shapes A to E from your chosen fabric in the quantities given below. The templates are sewing size, so allow a 5mm (¼in) seam allowance around each template when cutting the fabric. Trace around the plastic templates with a pencil. This pencil line is the sewing line.

Note that some of the templates are reversed for cutting. Flip the template over and mark the fabric in the usual manner. Reversed templates are shown (R).

SCRAP FABRIC
From the scrap squares, cut 432 triangles using Template A.

BACKGROUND FABRIC
From the background fabric cut the following shapes:
For the Blocks: You will need 432 shapes using Template B, 216 triangles using Template D and another 216 using Template DR (reversed).
For the Border Blocks: You will need 60 shapes using Template D, 60 using DR, 60 using E and 60 using the ER template.
For the Corner Blocks: You will need 4 shapes using Template D, 4 using DR, 4 using E, and 4 using the ER template.

STAR FABRIC
From the star fabric, set aside a 75cm (29½in) square for the binding and then cut the following:
For the Blocks: cut 216 shapes using

Template C and 216 using the CR template.
For the Border Blocks: 60 shapes using template C and 60 using the CR template.
For the Corner Blocks: 4 shapes using Template C and 4 using the CR template.

ASSEMBLING THE BLOCKS

Referring to the Block, Corner Block and Block Border Diagrams, assemble the blocks in the following way.

BLOCK
Join an A, B, C and D; then an A, B, CR and DR. Join these two units to make a quarter block. Make another quarter block and join it to the first to make a rectangle. Repeat this procedure to make another rectangle and join the two rectangles together to complete the square Block. Make a total of 54 square Blocks.

BORDER BLOCK
Join an E, C and D and then an ER, CR and DR. Join these to make a square. Make another square in the same way and join the two squares to form a rectangle. Make a total of 30 rectangular Border Blocks.

CORNER BLOCK
Join an E, C and D then an ER, CR and DR. Join the two triangles to make a square. Make four Corner Blocks.

JOINING THE BLOCKS

Press all blocks lightly. Lay out the blocks with six square blocks across and nine square blocks down. Join the blocks across in rows, then join the rows together.

FINISHED SIZE
- 250cm x 175cm (100in x 70in)

MATERIALS
- 432 x 8cm (3¼in) squares of fabric for pinwheel triangles
- 5m (5²⁄₃yd) of background fabric
- 2.8m (3yd) of fabric for the stars, or use various scraps. This includes 75cm (29⁵⁄₈in) square of star fabric for binding
- 5.5m (6⅓yd) backing fabric
- Batting to fit quilt plus 10cm (4in)
- Sewing thread
- Template plastic
- Sharp HB pencil
- Quilting thread
- General sewing supplies

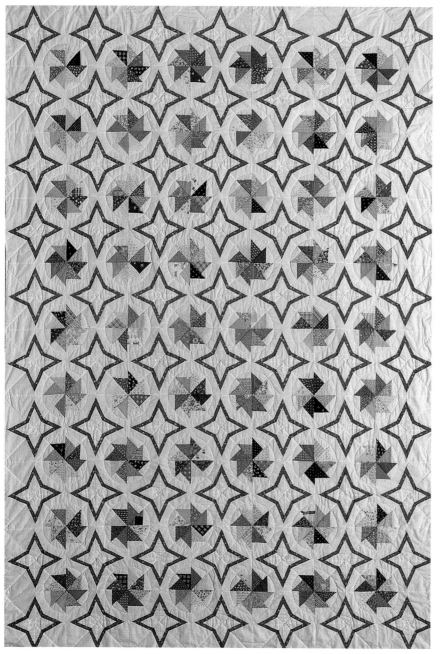

At this point, mark the quilting design. The quilt in the photograph has been stitched in the ditch and a circle sewn around the pinwheels.

QUILTING

Cut the selvedges off the backing fabric and cut the fabric in half. From one of the pieces cut two, 50cm (20in) strips the length of the fabric. Join these lengthwise to each side of the other long strip with a 5mm (¼in) seam allowance. Press the seams towards the centre.

Lay the backing right side down on your work surface, lay the batting on top and then the quilt top with right side up. Baste the three layers together in a 12cm (5in) grid, and quilt as desired. Remove the basting.

BINDING

Cut and sew a continuous strip of binding 6cm (2½in) wide. You will need a 9m (350in) length to go right around. (See 'Binding' on page 158 in the techniques section for instructions on creating a continuous bias strip.)

With wrong sides together, press the binding in half lengthwise, then unfold the strip. Begin on a long side of the quilt and, with right sides facing and raw edges together, sew the binding to the front of the quilt through all thicknesses, sewing 1cm in from the edge. Mitre the corners when you come to them. Trim the edges then fold the binding to the back of the quilt and slip stitch it into position.

Make two strips, each with nine rectangular Border Blocks, and join them to the long sides of the quilt. Make another two strips, each with six rectangular Border Blocks and one square Corner Block on each end. Join the strips to the top and bottom of the quilt.

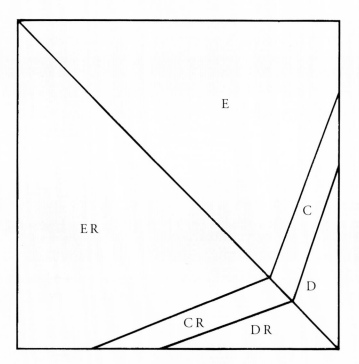

PINWHEEL AND
STAR PATTERN TEMPLATES

CORNER BLOCK DIAGRAM

For each block cut:

Templates E and ER: one of each from background fabric.

Templates C and CR: one of each from star fabric.

Templates D and DR: one of each from background fabric.

Make a total of four blocks.

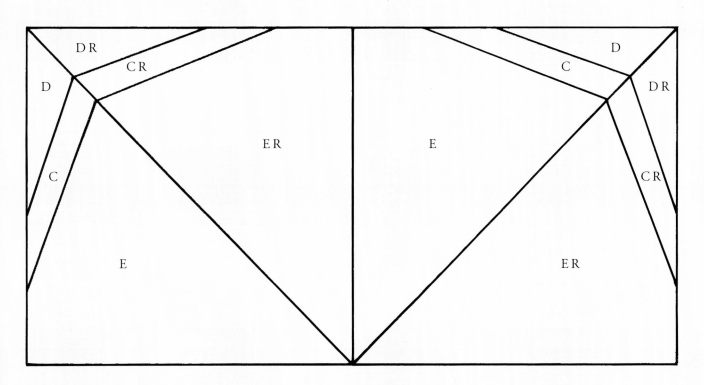

BORDER BLOCK DIAGRAM

For each block cut:

Templates E and ER: two of each from background fabric.

Templates C and CR: two of each from star fabric.

Templates D and DR: two of each from background fabric.

Make a total of 30 blocks.

144%

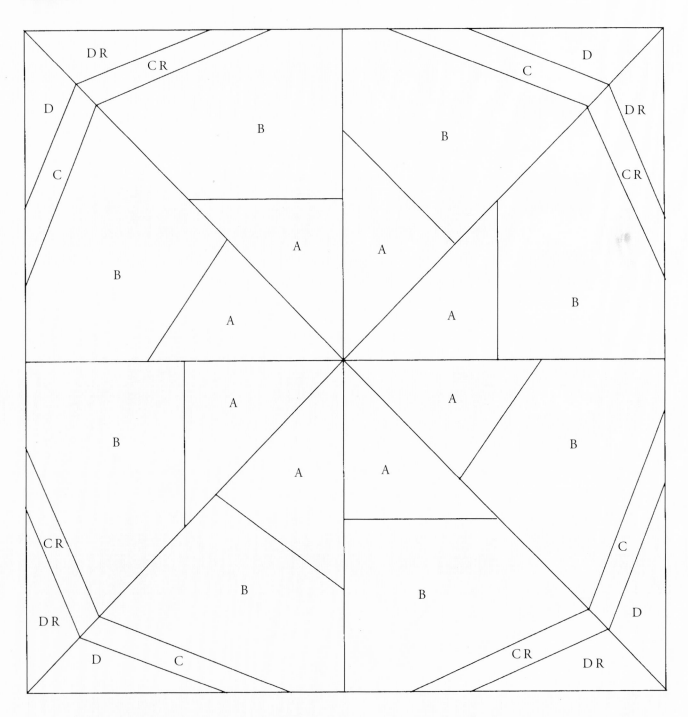

BLOCK DIAGRAM (25cm block)

For each block cut out:

Template A: eight from scrap fabric.

Template B: eight from background fabric.

Template C and CR: four of each from star fabric.

Template D and DR: four of each from background fabric.
                         Make a total of 54 blocks.

  144%

Seaside Memories

Bring the seaside home with this collage of shells and other found objects. Shell collages can also be used to decorate keepsake boxes, mirrors, picture frames and other items. Once you have perfected the technique, you are limited only by your imagination and your supply of shells.

FINISHED SIZE

- 40cm x 30cm (16in x 12in)

MATERIALS

- 40cm x 30cm (16in x 12in) pine board or tray
- Wattyl Water-Based Woodstain: Limestone
- 5cm (2in) brush
- Selection of shells in a variety of shapes and sizes
- 2 starfish
- Tilancia moss
- 15cm x 12cm x 4cm (6in x 12in x 1½in) block of florist's dry foam
- Glue gun
- Florist's wire, 20 gauge and 18 gauge
- 50cm x 5mm (½yd x ³⁄₁₆in) decorative cord
- Blu-Tack
- Tools: knife, cutters, pliers, scissors

Shells in a terracotta urn make an elegant candle holder.

PREPARATION

Prepare your wooden board by painting it with woodstain and allowing it to dry overnight. Scrub your selected shells and starfish in a bucket of soapy water, rinse them several times in clear water and leave them to dry thoroughly.

PLANNING THE DESIGN

Sort the large shells and other feature items from the smaller, filler shells. Place the painted board on a flat surface and arrange the large shells on the board without gluing them, moving them about until you are satisfied with the arrangement. If necessary, use Blu-Tack to hold the objects in place until you are ready to attach them permanently.

WIRING THE SHELLS

Some small shells don't need wiring so when you are satisfied with your design, decide which shells you will need to wire. For each of the larger shells and starfish take 25cm (10in) of the 18 gauge wire and bend it in half to create a loop. For the smaller shells, take 15cm (6in) of the 20 gauge wire, and again bend in half to create a loop. Attach the wire loops to the shells by placing a dot of glue inside or on the shell, depending how the shell will be placed in the arrangement. Position the wire onto the shell and hold it in place for a minute before setting aside. Keep a plate handy to lean the wired shells on.

ATTACHING THE SHELLS

Using enough glue to cover the bottom of the florist's foam, place the foam block in the centre of the board or wherever you intend to arrange the shells. Cover the foam with tilancia moss and fix the moss in place with several pieces of 20 gauge wire cut into 10cm (4in) lengths and bent into a hairpin shape. Attach large, flat shells (such as scallop shells) around the edges of the foam block by inserting the wire attached to them into the oasis, overlapping them as you go. Next position the large focal shell, then the starfish. Working with the points of the shells flowing in a neat line out from the focal point, position all the shells on the foam. Use the glue gun to place a small amount of glue on the edge of each of the small shells and slip them into any bare spaces. Continue until the foam is well covered. You may wish to put more moss around the shape to soften it. Curl the decorative cord through and around the design, fixing permanently with glue.

OTHER WAYS TO USE SHELLS

Shells can be a versatile addition to a floral arrangement. They are very effective when used in a table centre-piece. A talking point can be created by placing a few prized shells in a shallow float bowl and adding gardenias or camellias.

Shells and driftwood make an attractive bathroom display that will withstand damp conditions. Tilancia moss together with dried eucalyptus twigs and driftwood can form the basis of a wall plaque. Shells and starfish can then be used to complete the design.

A most attractive candle holder can be made by decorating a terracotta urn with shells and other found objects. Fill the urn with dry florist's foam and scoop a hole in the centre to accommodate a candle. Cover the foam with moss, then attach wired shells to the foam. Wire the large shells in first and place the smaller shells around it.

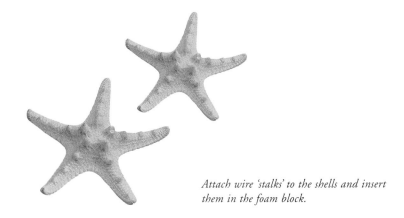

Attach wire 'stalks' to the shells and insert them in the foam block.

Doily Drama

A beautiful hand-crafted doily is the focal point for this dramatic coffee and cream cushion. Ribbons and machine-sewn embroidery have been used to extend and enhance the lace design. You will need some previous experience of machine embroidery and appliqué techniques.

PREPARATION

From the calico, cut a 35cm (14in) square for the cushion front, two rectangles 32cm x 35cm (12⅝in x 14in) for the cushion back and two fabric strips the width of the fabric and 20cm wide, for the outside frill.

From the coffee-coloured fabric, cut four 10cm (4in) squares for the appliqué shapes, and three fabric strips the width of the fabric and 12cm (4¾in) wide for the inside frill.

From the interfacing, cut four 10cm (4in) squares for backing the appliqué fabric. Iron the interfacing to the back of the four squares of coffee-coloured fabric.

From the iron on Pellon/fleece, cut a 35cm (14in) square and iron onto the wrong side of the cushion front.

Fold the cushion front into halves both ways to obtain the centre point. Rule these lines with a water-soluble blue pen. Again fold the front in halves both ways, but this time on the diagonal. Rule in the diagonals with the blue pen. The lines will be used for placement of the appliqué and machine embroidery.

Place the doily in the exact centre of the cushion front and pin it in place. Using matching thread, stitch the doily down around the edge and twice more in a circle working in towards the centre and following the doily lines.

STITCHING THE APPLIQUE

If you have a machine that has an embroidery unit attached, choose a suitable appliqué design and, using the placement lines you drew on the cushion, appliqué four designs 9cm (3½in) from the centre of the cushion using the lighter coffee-coloured thread (refer to the photograph).

Once your machine has stitched out the first row, place the appliqué fabric under the foot, inside the hoop, and stitch out the next three rows of straight stitching. Take the hoop out of the sewing machine and cut away the excess fabric by cutting around the design stitch line, close to the edge of the stitching. Place the hoop back into the sewing machine and complete the appliqué.

If you are doing the appliqué manually, cut out your design. Iron the design in place on the cushion front, then using a small zigzag stitch with a width of 3.0 and a density of 0.25, appliqué your design in place. The Pellon on the back of the cushion front will help give a quilted effect to your stitching. You may need to place paper as a stabiliser to help the layers feed through. If your machine has a built-in "dual feed" (walking foot) use this to ensure perfect fabric feeding, no matter how many layers of fabric there are.

ADDING THE MACHINE EMBROIDERY

Using a circular template with a diameter of 12cm (4¾in), draw in half circle shapes between each of the appliqué designs, extending out 6cm (2⅜in) along the diagonal lines into each corner. Use these half-circle shapes as guidelines for the machine embroidery.

Using paper as a backing, machine embroider a design with the darker coffee-coloured thread. Around the half circle lines, use a small satin stitch and on the outside of the semi-circle, embroider a small scallop which just touches the first row of embroidery. Repeat on the other three half circles.

Lower the dogs on your machine and, using a darning foot, free motion stipple the insides of these half circles to extend the doily design.

FINISHED SIZE

- 45cm (18in) square

MATERIALS

- 1m (1⅛yd) calico or cream homespun
- 50cm (½yd) coffee-coloured bem silk
- 10cm (4in) iron-on interfacing for backing appliqué
- 35cm (⅜yd) iron-on Pellon/fleece
- 25cm (¼yd) diameter coffee-coloured doily 30-weight, 100% cotton
- 50cm (½yd) of 6mm (¼in) tan ribbon
- 1 reel 30-weight, 100% cotton coffee coloured thread
- 1 reel 30-weight, 100% cotton dark coffee-coloured thread
- 1 reel 30-weight, 100% cotton cream thread
- Small quantity of polyester stuffing
- Cushion insert
- Water-soluble blue pen
- Small sharp scissors
- General sewing requirements

Thread the tan ribbon through the holes in the doily and tie a small bow on the diagonal.

MAKING UP
THE CUSHION

Join the calico frill pieces to form a circle, then fold the frill pieces in half lengthwise with wrong sides together and gather the frill up to fit the cushion. Repeat for the three pieces of coffee-coloured fabric.

With the raw edges of the frills and cushion together, and the frills to the centre of the cushion, pin first the smaller, coffee-coloured frill to the edge of the cushion front and then the larger, cream frill over the top. Make sure you have more gathers on the corners so they will sit well.

Turn under a 1cm (⅜in) hem on both of the backing pieces, then fold under another 5cm (2in) hem. Press firmly and stitch down. Overlap the two backing pieces with the hems in the centre and so that they make a 35cm (13¾in) square (the same size as the cushion front).

Then stitch down both sides to hold the pieces in place.

Pin all the frill pieces to the centre of the cushion front. With the right sides of the cushion front and back together, stitch around all four outside edges. Trim away the excess fabric and clip the corners. Turn the cushion right side out and press.

You'll achieve a well-shaped cushion if you first stuff the corners of the cushion with polyester stuffing until they are nicely rounded. Then place a suitable cushion insert through the back opening to complete your cushion.

Weighty Matters

Folk artists are classic recyclers and in this project ordinary electricity insulators from old power poles have been transformed into charming paperweights. The design could be painted on any round item – just enlarge or reduce the pattern to fit, or add a few extra hills and trees.

MATERIALS

- Ceramic electricity insulator or similar round-shaped item
- Black carbon transfer paper
- Tracing paper
- Stylus or empty ball point pen
- No 0 liner brush
- No 2 soft, pointed round brush (preferably pure sable)
- No 10 flat shader brush
- DecoArt Ultra Gloss acrylic enamel paints: Williamsburg Blue, Gloss White, Cranberry, True Blue, Christmas Green, Lemon Yellow, Sable Brown, Chocolate, Buttermilk, Christmas Red, Gloss Black, Hunter Green, Mustard

TIPS FOR USING DECOART ULTRA GLOSS

Because the surface is glazed ceramic and therefore shiny, ordinary artists' acrylics will not adhere successfully. You will need to use acrylic enamels — newly developed paints that clean up with water and are designed especially for use on shiny surfaces. They dry with a gloss finish. Always shake the paint well before using.

With acrylic enamels, it is essential to allow each stage to dry before applying the next. Shading cannot be done until the paint below is dry. If you attempt to paint one layer over another while the first is still wet, the paint will lift. Do not thin the paint with water.

PREPARATION

Wash and dry the insulator thoroughly. Trace both patterns from page 72 onto tracing paper. Using the black carbon paper and a stylus, trace on pattern No 1.

Be careful not to lean against the carbon, as it comes off a shiny surface very easily.

STEP ONE

SKY AND CLOUDS

Load a very soft, small round brush with Williamsburg Blue and paint the sky, gently brushing on the blue all the way around the paperweight and down between the mountain areas. Loading the round brush again with blue, flatten it out and pick up Gloss White on the flattened side of the brush. Then paint the clouds in big and little C strokes, using a pushing motion. With the left-over white still on the brush, soften the edges of the clouds.

MOUNTAINS, PADDOCKS AND FOREGROUND

The hills and paddocks may need two coats. Allow at least half an hour's drying time between each coat.

Mix a soft mauve colour with Cranberry and Williamsburg Blue and paint the row of mountains marked 'A' on pattern

Step-by-step painting guide.

Detail of the shed and surrounds.

No 1. Paint in the 'B' mountains with Cranberry and True Blue and use a mix of Christmas Green, Lemon Yellow and Sable Brown in equal parts to paint the 'C' hills. Use a mix of equal parts Chocolate and Lemon Yellow to paint the 'D' paddocks. Dab Lemon Yellow on the 'E' paddocks. Using the same mix as for the 'C' hills but with a little more Lemon Yellow added, paint the 'C' area in the foreground.

STEP TWO

Using pattern No 2 on page 72, transfer the tree trunks, roads, houses and shed. Do not transfer the tops of the trees, bushes, sheep or fences as these are to be done freehand later.

Using the pointed round brush, paint the tree trunks in Chocolate and the front of the shed in Buttermilk with a touch of Chocolate. The side of the shed, roof and door are all Chocolate. Allow to dry and then paint some thin strokes in Buttermilk on the front of the roof.

The house walls are Buttermilk, while the roof is a mix of equal parts Christmas Red and Chocolate. The chimney is Gloss Black and the windows Chocolate.

Let these dry and then paint thin strokes of Buttermilk on the roof. Use Buttermilk to paint a little smoke coming out of the chimney.

SHADING

Using a flat shader brush, corner load in Chocolate, blend well on the palette and shade behind the line of 'D' and 'E' hills and paddocks. You will be shading on the green hills and also on the brown and yellow paddocks.

FREEHAND DETAILS

All the bushes and tops of the trees are pushed on with a pointed round brush. Load the tip of the brush and push the colour on. The bushes are Hunter Green. The tops of the trees are Hunter Green and Mustard. All the fences are painted with a liner brush in Chocolate with a touch of Gloss Black added. The sheep are painted with Buttermilk, pushing the paint on with a

thick glob. Allow to dry thoroughly. Under all the sheep and the trees paint a little Chocolate as a shade area. Allow to dry thoroughly.

TRIM

To finish off the top edge, use the wooden end of the round brush and dot with Cranberry. If desired, add the recipient's name using a liner brush.

FINISHING

Follow the directions on the back of the Ultra Gloss bottle for setting the paint. Do not use temperatures higher than those indicated on the bottle. Reduce 10 to 20 degrees Celsius for a fan-forced oven. Never heatset in a microwave, only in a conventional oven. Always heat-set in a well-ventilated area with the exhaust fan running. Air the oven afterwards. If you have a small portable oven, it is best to reserve this for heat-setting, rather than using your kitchen oven.

WEIGHTY MATTERS
Design Outline

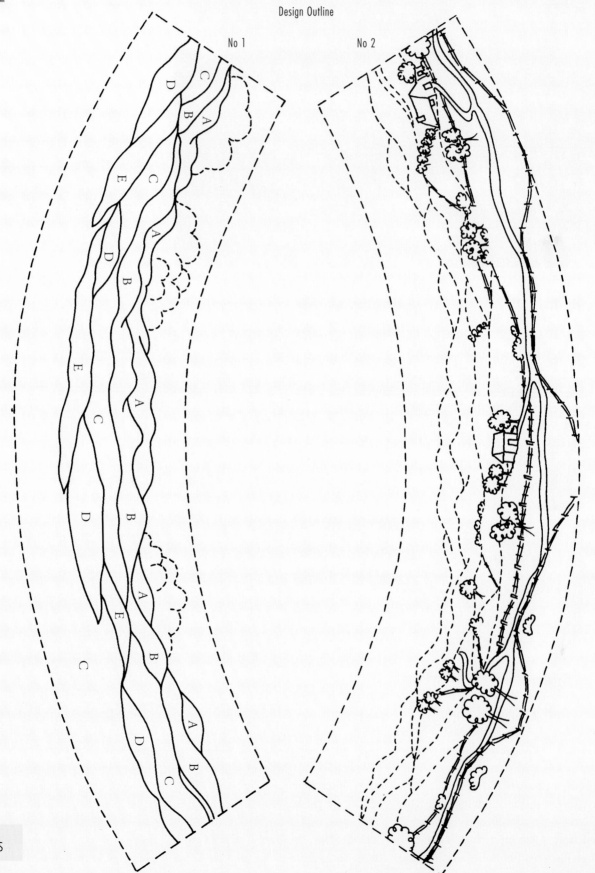

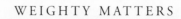

Floral Keepsake

Flannel flowers, Albany daisies, tea tree, fairy stasis, cassinia and assorted fine leaves were mounted behind glass on a padded fabric backing, to make this elegant keepsake box. However, many other flowers are also suitable for pressing.

FINISHED SIZE

- 39cm x 29cm (15½in x 11½in)

MATERIALS

- 39cm x 29cm (15½in x 12in) wooden box with recessed lid
- Glass to fit inside recessed lid
- Thin acrylic edging to secure glass
- 45cm x 35cm (18in x 14in) backing fabric
- Piece of batting to fit inside lid recess
- 2 pieces of cardboard, one to fit the recessed lid and one approx. 4cm (1½in) larger all round
- Flowers, leaves and stems
- Blotting paper
- Nappy liners or absorbent tissue
- Flower press or telephone book
- Good quality craft glue
- Cocktail stick or small paintbrush
- Tweezers and dressmaking pins
- Scissors
- Soft brush

Assemble your dried flowers and other equipment.

PRESSING
THE FLOWERS

The best time of the day to pick your flowers and foliage is early morning on a dry day. Pick only material that is free from blemishes.

Sort your flowers, leaves and stems into species or colour groups, making sure they are all free from moisture. Lay the flowers out in rows on blotting paper making sure none of the plant material is touching. Cover each layer with a nappy liner or absorbent tissue as you go. Sort the leaves from the stems and lay them on separate sheets of blotting paper and cover.

Place a heavy object, such as a sheet of glass or a telephone book over the absorbent material. For smaller pieces you can use flower presses available from craft stores.

The length of time plant material takes to dry depends on the thickness of the material and the humidity of the air. Check after about three weeks and then every few days after that.

PREPARATION

Cut the backing fabric and batting to the same size as the recessed lid. Mark the centre of the backing material and iron out any fold lines or wrinkles. Cut one piece of cardboard to the size of the recess and mark the centre, then rule horizontal and vertical lines through the centre to act as grid lines for placing your material. Cut another piece of cardboard approximately 4cm (1½in) larger.

Keeping in mind the colour and the proportion of the recessed area of the lid, choose the pressed flowers you wish to use and lay them out on a tray.

ASSEMBLING THE DESIGN

Experiment with your design on the smaller piece of cardboard, using the ruled lines to help you centre your design. Using tweezers, start by positioning the background flowers. Slide the flowers around to obtain a pleasing balance and outline. Arrange your main flowers on top of the background flowers. Always select your best specimens for the focal points of your design. Position the filler leaves, smaller flowers and sprays to complement the central flowers and to fill in the gaps. As the design is not fixed at this point, now is the time to change your choice of pressed flowers or your design until you achieve one that you are pleased with.

TRANSFERRING THE DESIGN

You are now ready to transfer and glue your arrangement onto the backing fabric. Place your backing fabric onto the larger piece of cardboard, smooth out any wrinkles and secure it with pins or removable tape.

When fixing your arrangement with craft glue, it is important to remember to use the glue sparingly. Any excess glue not covered by your pressed material will be shiny and appear magnified under the glass.

Slide a background flower from the cardboard and apply a small amount of glue to the back using a small brush or cocktail stick. Fix it to the corresponding position on the backing fabric. Transfer and glue all the background flowers in this way, then transfer your central flowers. Using tweezers, lift the edges of the fixed pieces and 'tuck in' the complementary fillers. Allow sufficient time for the glue to dry.

ASSEMBLING THE LID

Clean the glass, making sure there are no smears or fingerprints. Using a soft brush, remove any specks or loose bits from your backing fabric.

Place the batting into the recess of the lid. Remove the backing fabric with your design attached from the cardboard and place it on top of the batting.

Position the glass over your finished design. While maintaining maximum pressure over your work, apply the acrylic edging to secure the glass in place.

First arrange the design on cardboard using tweezers to pick up the plant material.

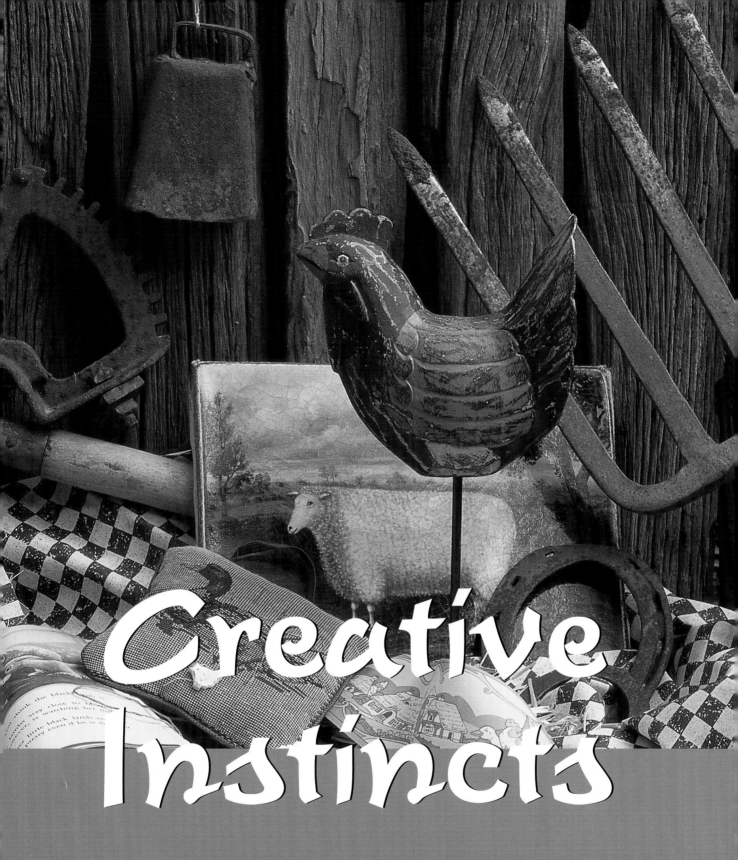

Creative Instincts

There is no limit to the types of material, or the tools and methods that can be employed in creating decorative and useful craft pieces. In this section we highlight a wide range of methods and designs that, with a little imagination, can be applied to many other projects.

A Touch of Gold

*Goldwork, or metal thread embroidery, was once the preserve
of the church and the very rich. Today, however, a wide variety
of affordable threads that simulate the opulence of real gold
and silver, are available and are easy to work with.*

PREPARATION

Place the embroidery carbon on top of the black linen, carbon side down. On top of the carbon, place the design outline traced from pages 82 and 83. Centre the design and make sure it is parallel with the fabric grain. Pin all surfaces together around the edges.

Pressing reasonably firmly with the 2B pencil, trace accurately over all design lines, dots and other markings. Be careful not to move the design as you work and resist the temptation to check progress while you are tracing.

Remove the design sheet and carbon. Place the linen on top of the ecology cloth and baste the fabrics together around the design area and around all edges. Mount the traced linen and ecology cloth in a tapestry frame and tighten until taut.

EMBROIDERING THE CENTRAL MOTIF

Begin by working the centre design in which the gold cord is couched to the fabric with gold machine thread.

Thread the darning needle with a single 60cm (23½in) strand split from the twisted gold cord. Tie a knot in the end of the strand. Thread a straw needle with gold machine thread and tie a knot in the end.

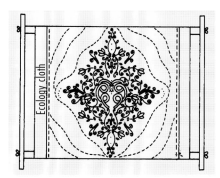

Using the stiletto, make a small hole through the linen and ecology cloth at dot 'A' on the Couching Diagram on page 81. Bring the darning needle and gold cord up through the hole. Leave the needle attached to the cord and bring the straw needle and thread up next to the cord, about 1mm along design line 'O'. Bring the machine thread over the top of the cord and then take the needle through to the back of the work on the other side of the cord. Continue in this manner with stitches approximately 1.5mm (¹⁄₁₆in) apart. Come up and go down as close to the cord as possible, so that the stitches will be almost invisible. The cord should be held with one hand to keep it straight and lying next to the design line. Cord tension should not be too tight or too slack, but should lie smoothly on the surface of the linen.

With the cord lying at all times just inside design line 'O', continue couching the gold cord until you reach dot 'B', then take the darning needle and cord to the back of the work. Snip the cord, leaving an end of about 1cm (³⁄₈in). Fold the end back over the worked area. Bring the straw needle to the back of the work and stitch through the ecology cloth only, securing this end.

Following the couching instructions above, couch five cords side by side with just a needle distance between, starting at dots 'C', 'D', 'E' and 'F'. You have now completed the left half of the central design. Repeat all of the above for the right half of the central motif.

Thread a length of Kreinik braid into the darning needle. Make a hole with the stiletto at 'H' and couch the braid following the outside design line 'K'. Take the braid to the back of the work at dot '1'

Place the linen on top of the ecology cloth and tack the fabric together around the design area and around all edges. Mount the linen and ecology cloth in a tapestry frame and tighten until taut.

FINISHED SIZE

- 25cm x 31cm (10in x 12½in) (embroidery only)

MATERIALS

- 40cm (16in) square Jacquard or plain black linen, cut on the grain
- 50cm (20in) ecology cloth or homespun
- Pure silk embroidery thread, two packets gold
- Cotton on Creations Jap gold, 1 skein (608)
- Kreinik Metallics heavy braid, two reels gold (32)
- Rajmahal Smooth Purl Sadi thread, gold
- 2.5m x 2mm (2³⁄₄yds x ¹⁄₁₆in) twisted gold craft cord (should have three or four strands in the twist)
- Chenille needles (assorted sizes)
- Straw needles (sizes 5–10)
- Gütermann No 50 cotton machine thread, gold (0847)
- Embroiderer's carbon in yellow or white (not dressmaker's carbon)
- Stiletto
- Large-eyed darning needle
- 15cm (6in) square gold-coloured felt
- 23 Hotspotz 3mm (¹⁄₈in) beads, gold (P3-20)
- Mill Hill glass seed beads: one packet colour 00221
- 60cm (24in) tapestry frame
- 2B pencil

*Overcast felt flowers, couching
and satin stitch.*

LEAVES

Using a straw needle threaded with one strand of silk thread, satin stitch each leaf, going 14 times into the same holes. Lay the thread to achieve a leaf shape.

Thread up a chenille needle with two, 50cm (20in) lengths of Jap gold and knot the ends together. Make a small hole with the stiletto at the base of each leaf. Bring the chenille needle up to the front of the work. Thread a straw needle with gold machine thread. Bring the needle up at point 'C' of the leaf (see Embroidery Diagram). Make a lazy daisy loop with the Jap gold. Make one couching stitch at the point of the leaf, over the Jap gold loop. Take the chenille needle to the back of the work, down the same hole you came up. Place one couching stitch on either side of the leaf centre. Bring the straw needle to the base of the leaf. Thread a Mill Hill bead and stitch to the base. The Jap gold loop should surround the satin stitching to keep the leaf shape. Do not pull the Jap gold tight. The Jap gold can be carried for short distances across the back of the work from leaf to leaf until the thread is used up or begins to wear.

and bring it up again at dot '2'. Continue in this manner to the top of the design. Couch the braid in a loop as shown on the Couching Diagram and continue couching the braid down the right-hand, outside edge of the motif.

Attach large gold Hotspotz beads at the positions marked by dots on the design outline on pages 82–83.

STEMS AND CURLS

Couch Kreinik braid to all stems and curls, but not to flowers, flower stems, or the four groups of three curls marked 'P' on the design outline. Stitch on the large gold beads at the dots. Using one strand of the twisted gold cord (as for the central motif), couch the four groups of curls marked 'P'.

FLOWERS

From the felt, and using the templates given on page 82, cut out the flower shapes 1 to 10 and the centre petals 1 to 10. Place the felt flowers in position on the linen and overcast with gold machine thread and a straw needle. Position and overcast the corresponding centre petal shapes.

Thread the darning needle with Kreinik braid and couch the braid around the flower by coming up the stem, around the centre panel, up the outer petal to 'B' (see Embroidery Diagram). Go to the back of the work, coming out again at 'C'. Work around the petal to 'D' and end off.

Cut a length of smooth Sadi thread so that it fits neatly between the base and the end of the centre petal. Sadi is actually a coiled spring and must be handled with care as it does not regain its shape if stretched. Thread up a fine straw needle with machine thread. Bring the needle up at the base, pass the needle through the centre of the coil as if it were a bead, then take the needle to the back of the work at the tip of the petal. Repeat this process until the centre petal is covered with lengths of Sadi. Around six or seven lengths should cover this petal. Do not try to cram too many lengths in; they should lie side by side. The lengths will decrease as you work out from the centre. With the same fine straw needle and machine thread, stitch Mill Hill beads one by one over the left and right hand petals, keeping inside the Kreinik braid surrounds.

FINISHING

❖

The goldwork is now complete. Remove it from the tapestry frame and take out the basting stitches.

Goldwork cannot be pressed, although you can carefully iron the surrounding fabric. The work can be framed or, as shown, mounted in the lid of a custom-made box.

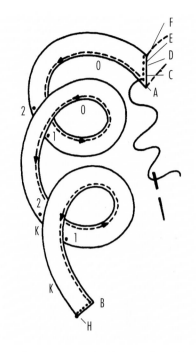

Couching Diagram, for the central motif

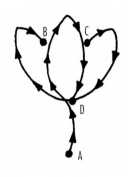

Embroidery Diagram, for the flowers

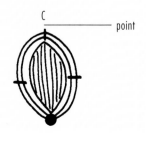

Embroidery Diagram, for the leaves

B

A TOUCH OF GOLD
Design Outline

FLOWER AND
CENTRE PETAL
TEMPLATES

 SS

Line up A lines and B lines
to make full pattern

Fern Magic

The technique of spatter painting over ferns was used in the late nineteenth century to decorate chests, tables, screens and cutlery boxes. This easy method can be used to paint any wooden article that has a large enough area to accommodate a pleasing arrangement of the ferns.

THE FRAME

❖

Disassemble the screen. Cover work area with newspaper, and paint the frame and mouldings with Pine Green, using a sponge brush. Allow to dry. Mix two parts Storm Blue, one part Warm White and one part Pthalo Blue and repaint the mouldings and frame with the blue mixture (see Step 1). Allow to dry.

Lightly sand to reveal the green undercoat. Rub with steel wool until smooth. To achieve a gleaming finish, apply some beeswax using steel wool (see Step 2).

THE PANELS

❖

Using the sponge brush and Pine Green, paint the panels and allow to dry. Lightly sand the area and apply a second coat.

Flatten the ferns by placing them between two sheets of brown paper and ironing them with a hot iron. Arrange the ferns as desired on the panels of the screen (see Step 3).

Mix blue paint as before but use two parts of Warm White instead of one. Thin the paint until it will spatter easily and test it on the newspaper.

Load the paint sparingly onto the nail brush, wipe off any excess on the paper towel or sponge. Aim the bristles at the area to be spattered and run your finger along the bristles to make paint flick onto the panels over the ferns. Continue until you have the desired coverage (see Step 3). Remove the ferns and allow the paint to dry before placing the panels into the frame and fitting the hinges and mouldings (see Step 4).

MATERIALS

- Craftwood firescreen
- Sponge brush or wide brush for background painting
- Jo Sonja's Artists' Acrylics: Storm Blue, Pthalo Blue, Warm White, Pine Green
- Assorted fern fronds (a variety of different ferns with an open leaf work best)
- Nail brush
- Paper towel or sponge for removing excess paint from brush
- Brown paper
- Newspaper
- Iron
- Fine sandpaper
- Steel wool
- Beeswax
- Tack cloth

1. *Protect your work area with sheets of newspaper or work outdoors. Paint the frame of the screen green, allow it to dry then apply a coat of blue. A sponge brush gives a smooth finish free from brushstrokes.*

2. *Allow the paint to dry thoroughly then lightly sand in places to reveal the green undercoat. Finish by rubbing smooth with steel wool and applying beeswax, again with steel wool.*

3. *Arrange the ferns on the panels. Thin the paint to a consistency that will spatter and load sparingly onto a nail brush. Remove excess by brushing on a paper towel or sponge. Spatter the paint over the ferns by running your finger over the bristles with the brush aimed at the panel.*

4. *Remove ferns to reveal your spatter pattern.*

3-D Effects

*Our Purple-Crowned Lorikeet makes an ideal subject for repoussé,
the traditional découpage technique in which part of the cut-out design
is raised from the surface with mastic. A knowledge of basic
découpage techniques is needed for this project.*

Répousse, in conjunction with traditional découpage, can be used to decorate a variety of different objects and surfaces.

FINISHED SIZE

- 30cm x 18cm (11³/₄in x 7¹/₈in)

MATERIALS

- Craftwood or pine timber plaque
- Woodsealer
- Artists' acrylic paint (for background and edges)
- Images
- Fine, curved cuticle scissors
- Liquitex Gloss Medium & Varnish or Jo Sonja All Purpose Sealer
- Soft lead pencil
- Soft, foam table mat available from chain stores
- Air-drying moulding material or mastic (such as DAS Pronto, available from art and craft suppliers)
- Burnisher (tool with spoon-like shape at one end and fine point at other, such as used by potters and leather workers)
- Aquadhere and Clag glues
- ³/₄in flat brush
- No 0000 very fine brush
- Sea sponge
- Water and household detergent
- Cotton buds
- Tack cloth
- No 600 and 1000 wet-and-dry sandpapers
- Varnish (such as Wattyl Speed Clear Satin)
- No 0000 steel wool
- Safety equipment (such as a mask for applying varnishes)

PREPARATION

Sand the plaque until smooth and seal with one coat of woodsealer. Apply two coats of the background colour of your choice (FolkArt Acrylic Teal Blue, No 717 was used in the plaque illustrated) and seal again.

Seal the front of the image with two thin layers of sealer and carefully cut out the image (see Step 1). Paint the edges of the image with a very fine brush, using colours that match the image.

SHAPING THE LORIKEET

Hold the image to be sculptured up to a window and lightly outline in pencil on the wrong side of those areas to be raised.

Lay the image face down on the mat and, using the spoon end of the burnisher, gently press down on the back of the image following the pencil marks to create an indentation (see Step 2). Stretch the paper slightly without wrinkling it. Press firmly just in from the edges so they curl upwards. Work on a small area at a time, pressing and shaping areas to be raised.

APPLYING THE MASTIC

Knead the mastic until it is smooth and pliable, then fashion pieces into shapes that will fit the areas to be filled. To achieve correct perspective, use more mastic underneath the parts of the design that will be closest to the viewer, but make sure the mastic does not overfill the area.

Mix two parts Aquadhere to one part Clag and apply to back of image (see Step 3). Lay mastic pieces in place, working quickly while the glue is still tacky. Before turning the image over, apply another coat of glue to both mastic and paper.

SCULPTING THE IMAGE

Very carefully turn the filled image over and position it on the prepared plaque.

1. *To cut small interior areas, make a hole in the paper with the point of the scissors, bring the blade up under the image and swivel the paper around the point of the blades.*

2. *Working with the image face down, follow the pencilled outlines of the areas to be raised with the end of the burnisher, pressing and rubbing to create indentations. Rub gently so the paper is stretched without wrinkling and press more firmly around the edges so that they curl upwards.*

3. *Apply glue to the back of the image and lay the mastic into the indentations. Use more mastic in the parts of the image that will be nearest the viewer, less in those areas further away. Press gently into place with the burnisher.*

4. *Use the burnisher and your fingers to press and mould the image. Follow the outlines of the image to form indentations in the mastic beneath and create a three dimensional effect.*

It is a good idea to cover the image with a damp paper towel and leave for ten minutes. Using the fine end of the burnisher, press the edges down. Then start 'sculpturing' the image using burnisher to follow the outlines of the image and make indentations into the mastic beneath (see Step 4). Commence sculpturing at the centre of the image easing out towards the edges. Indentations should flow naturally from higher areas to lower ones. For the lorikeet, for example, the outline of the wings and

the feathers were followed to achieve a realistic, three dimensional look. The branch in the foreground was also raised.

When you are happy with the sculpting, make sure that the edges are stuck down firmly. Clean up before the mastic has time to dry, wiping away any excess mastic with a dampened sea sponge and cotton buds. It may be necessary to neaten the edges of the image with a little paint and a fine brush. Leave to dry and harden.

VARNISHING

Once the piece has hardened commence varnishing. Apply about ten coats of varnish to raised areas taking care not to let varnish accumulate in the indentations. The background images to be left flat (leaves and fine branches in this case) should be varnished until sunk. Sand the raised areas delicately taking care not to sand the images back too far.

Allow three hours drying time between each coat of varnish. Use a tack cloth to remove dust between coats. Wet sandpaper with water mixed with a little detergent. Start sanding with the No 600 sandpaper and finish with the No 1000. The background should have a smooth, satin finish.

FINISHING

For extra definition, highlight the highest raised area with a coat of gloss varnish, or polish with No 0000 steel wool to achieve a shiny finish.

The finished piece will take several weeks to cure so handle the plaque with care during this time.

Country Garden Cushion

Add a touch of country to your patio or garden furniture with embroidered and appliquéd cushion covers. Featuring silk threads and buttons, this naive design can be stitched on either ecru or camel Klostern fabric to create two different looks.

FINISHED SIZE

- Appliquéd piece — 32cm x 27cm (12⅝in x 10⅝in)
  Cushion — 36cm x 29cm (14¼in x 11½in)

MATERIALS

- 40cm x 115cm (16in x 45in) of background fabric
- 29cm x 35cm (11½in x 14in) ecru or camel Klostern fabric
- Cushion insert to fit cover 36cm x 29cm (14¼in x 11½in) approx.
- Scraps of fabric for appliqué
- 20cm (8in) Vliesofix
- 5 x 10mm (⅜in) buttons
- 1 x 5mm (³⁄₁₆in) button for birdhouse
- Charms of your choice
- No 22 tapestry needle
- No 13 chenille needle
- Water-soluble pen
- Pencil
- General sewing requirements

CAMEL FABRIC

- Gum Nuts Silk Jewel threads: one skein each of Dk Jade, Med. Jasper, Dk Jasper, Dk Topaz
- Gum Nuts Silk Buds threads: One skein each of Yellow and 949

ECRU FABRIC

Colours for the ecru embroidery fabric appear in the instructions in brackets.

- Gum Nut Silk Jewel threads: Lt Amethyst, Med. Turquoise, Lt Garnet, Lt Jade, Lt Jasper, Med. Topaz
- Gum Nuts Silk Buds threads: 945 And 745.

PREPARATION

Thread a tapestry needle with one strand of Gum Nuts Silk Buds thread 949 (945) and hem stitch 1.5cm (⅝in) in from the top left-hand corner of the Klostern fabric. Stitching this line enables you to fray edges when the work is completed.

Please note that one strand of thread is used throughout this project. Part of the charm of a naive design is its 'raw' appearance, so do not be too fussy about making your stitches look perfectly even.

LETTERING

Following the graph on the pattern on page 93, begin embroidering the lettering, four holes in and four down from the top left-hand corner. With the tapestry needle threaded with Gum Nuts Silk Jewel thread: Dk Jade (Lt Jade), work the lettering in back stitch.

APPLIQUE

Trace and transfer all shapes from the pattern onto the smooth side of the Vliesofix paper. The templates for the watering can and sun have been drawn in reverse so that when they are ironed onto the fabric, they will face the correct way. Roughly cut around each shape.

Place the rough side of the Vliesofix onto the wrong side of the chosen fabric and iron into position. Now cut around the pencil line and peel off the backing paper (see Step 1). Position your pieces onto the Klostern fabric using the pattern and the photograph as a guide for placement and iron each piece in place.

EMBROIDERY

Thread the chenille needle with one strand of Dk Jasper (Lt Jasper) and work a small running stitch close to the edges of each appliqué piece (see Step 2). When embroidering, treat the Klostern fabric as a closely woven piece of fabric rather than trying to work the stitches from hole to hole (although this will occur occasionally).

Using the water-soluble pen, transfer stems and flowers from the pattern on page 92 onto the Klostern. Refer to page 92 for the colours of the various motifs.

Sew the buttons into position and place a French knot in the centre of all other flowers. Work lazy daisy stitches around the buttons and the French knots. Work the stems in stem stitch and the leaves in lazy daisy stitch (see Step 3). Work the rays of the sun in stem stitch.

Using the photograph below as a guide, sew the charms in place, sew the small button onto the birdhouse. Finish by sponging any marks out with cold water.

SEWING THE CUSHION

From the background fabric cut two rectangular pieces 37cm x 30cm (14½in x 12in) for the cushion back and one piece 45cm x 37cm (17¾in x 14½in) for the cushion front.

Lay the background fabric for the front on the work surface, right side up, centre the embroidered Klostern on top of it and tack it in place. Starting at the bottom right-hand corner, work a running stitch all the way round through both the background and the Klostern fabrics.

Sew a double hem along one 37cm side of each back piece. Place the front, right side up, on the work surface and place the two backs, right sides down, on top with the hemmed edges overlapping in the centre, so that the back fits the front exactly. Baste then machine-stitch the pieces together all the way round, neaten the seams, trim the corners and turn cushion right side out. Press carefully. For a well-filled appearance stuff the corners of the cushion with extra filling before placing the cushion insert inside.

1. *Transfer the pattern onto the smooth side of the Vliesofix paper. Roughly cut around each shape, position on the wrong side of the fabric, iron into place and then cut out along the design lines.*

2. *The appliqué pieces are first ironed onto the background fabric and then a decorative running stitch is worked around each piece.*

3. *To make the daisies, sew on the buttons and work lazy daisy stitches around them. Work the stems in stem stitch and the leaves in lazy daisy stitch.*

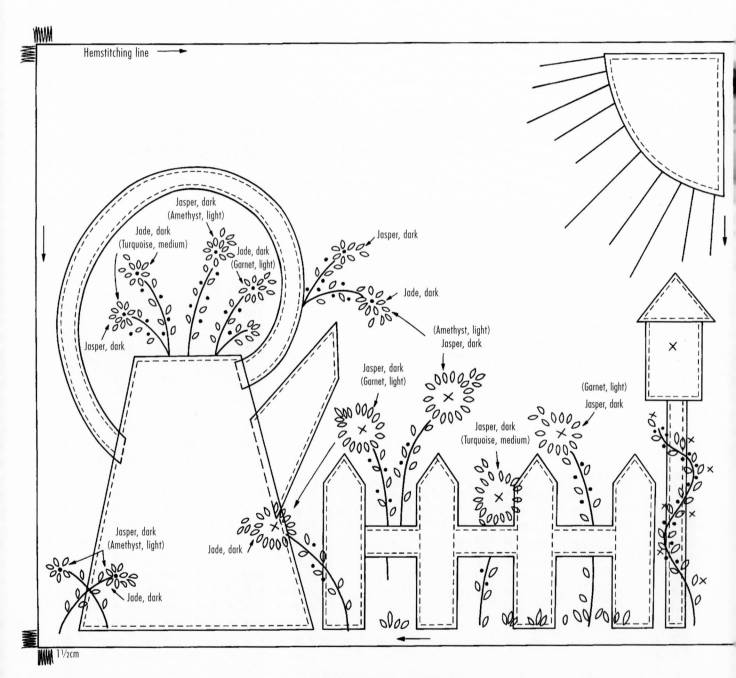

Hemstitching line →

Jasper, dark
(Amethyst, light)

Jade, dark
(Turquoise, medium)

Jade, dark
(Garnet, light)

Jasper, dark

Jasper, dark

Jade, dark

(Amethyst, light)
Jasper, dark

Jasper, dark
(Garnet, light)

(Garnet, light)
Jasper, dark

Jasper, dark
(Turquoise, medium)

Jasper, dark
(Amethyst, light)

Jade, dark

Jade, dark

1½cm

COUNTRY GARDEN
Layout Diagram and Colour Guide

166%

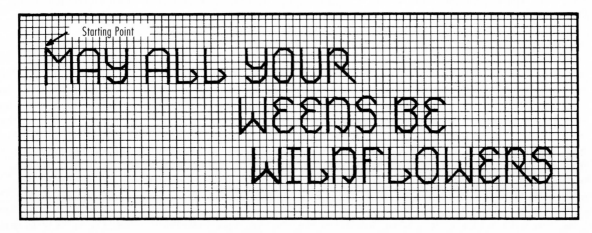

LETTERING GRAPH

 SS

WATERING CAN
TEMPLATE

SUN
TEMPLATE

166%

Sweet Dreams

It is very easy to turn white cotton sheets into luxury bed linen with the addition of embroidered borders. Use decorative machine stitching and white or white and cream thread, to create sheets and pillowcases that will give pleasure to all who sleep on them.

PREPARATION

Select pillow cases that have an extended outside edge and a sheet that has a return on the top edge. Treat areas to be stitched with liquid fabric stabiliser according to the manufacturer's instructions. Dry linen out of the sun and iron flat, true to the grain.

THE PILLOWCASE

With the ruler and water-soluble pen rule two parallel lines, 1.5cm (⅝in) apart, around the inside edge of the pillow case.

Select the 120 wing needle and a stitch that best resembles hem stitching. Most top-of-the-range machines have a variety of stitches designed to be used with a wing needle, but if you do not have one of these, select a stitch that goes back and forth in the same hole several times to not only punch a hole in the fabric, but to seal it with thread as well. Stitches like top stitch or stretch stitch will give a similar effect. Using white cotton thread, stitch around the entire inside edge of the pillow case, pivoting at the corners. Move 1.5cm (⅝in) closer to the outside edge and sew a second row of hem stitching in the same manner as before.

From the back and using the small, sharp scissors, cut away one layer of fabric between the two rows of hem stitching (see Step 1).

Change to a 75 needle and select a small, filled-in satin stitch scallop. Use either cream thread as shown on the pillow case in the photo, or white as shown on the sheet. Line the needle up

with the outside edge of the hem stitching, but not over the holes punched with the wing needle, and stitch around the edge of the row of the hem stitching. Repeat on the other side.

Carefully wash out the fabric stabiliser with warm water and lay the pillow case flat to dry out of the sun. When dry, press using a spray starch and set aside.

THE SHEET

On the top return of the sheet, come up 8cm (3¼in) from the bottom edge and rule a straight line across the entire edge. This provides a guide for the embroidery pattern. Select a deep decorative pattern and the white thread and sew across the width (see Step 2).

Rule a line on either side of this decorative pattern, 1cm (⅜in) away from it and parallel. Select the same satin stitch scallop that you used on the pillow case and sew along both guidelines. The scallops can be stitched in either cream, as on the pillow case in the photograph, or in white as shown on the sheet.

Change to the 120 wing needle and white thread. Using the same hem stitch as on the pillow case, stitch along the bottom edge of the return.

Change to a 75 needle and thread it with white or cream according to your design. Align the needle on the outside edge of the hem stitch below the hemming. Using the same satin stitch as before, stitch along the edge of the hem stitch.

Rinse the stabiliser out of the top edge of the sheet, dry out of the sun and iron flat with spray starch.

MATERIALS

- 1 single or double flat white bed sheet
- 1 or 2 plain pillow cases
- 1 reel of white cotton thread
- 1 reel of cream cotton thread
- Wing 120 machine needle
- Normal 75 machine needle
- Sew Stable liquid fabric stabiliser
- Water-soluble fabric pen
- Ruler
- General sewing requirements

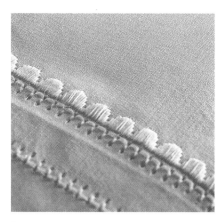

1. *Cut away the underneath layer of fabric between the two rows of hem stitching. Line the needle up against the outside edge of the stitching, but not over the holes already punched, and sew a satin stitch scallop.*

2. *Stitch an embroidery pattern. Leaving a 1cm gap, sew the scallop on either side.*

Temari Treasure

Since ancient times, the Japanese have used colourful thread-covered balls as festive decorations. The craft of Temari, involves intricate weaving and winding and requires patience and nimble fingers, but the final result is worth the effort. This stunning design is called Dancing Diamonds.

PREPARATION

Check that the surface of the ball is smooth and gently sand if necessary. Dents and bumps will affect the shape of the finished ball. Wind the green knitting yarn tightly around the ball in a random fashion. Turning the ball as you wrap to avoid overlapping the wool too many times in one direction which will create a football shape. As you wind, keep the ball as smoothly round as possible. When no polystyrene shows through the wool wrapping, hold the end of the wool against the ball and begin wrapping in the same manner with the green sewing cotton, until the ball is totally covered. Secure the cotton end by making a few big stitches into the surface of the ball and trimming the excess thread.

MARKING THE BALL INTO DIVISIONS

THE NORTH POLE

Push a pin through the end of the paper strip and into the ball. Note the colour of this pin which marks the north pole. Bring the paper down, passing it underneath the ball and back up to the pin to measure the circumference. Holding the paper firmly against the ball, cut off the end so that the strip is the exact length of the circumference. Still with the paper

attached to the ball, fold the paper accurately in half and in half again to make quarters and cut a small notch on one side of the paper at both folded edges.

THE SOUTH POLE

Open up the paper, wrap it around the ball and place a pin in the ball at the halfway notch to mark the south pole. Use a different coloured pin and note the colour.

THE EQUATOR

Still with the paper attached to the ball at the north pole, go to the one quarter notch between the two poles and place a pin there. This marks a point on the equator. With the paper still attached to the ball at the north pole, move the paper about one eighth of the way around the ball and place a pin at the quarter notch. Continue moving the paper and placing the pins until eight pins mark the equator. If possible use the same coloured pins for all eight equator points.

Remove the marking paper but keep the north pole pin in place. Fold the paper into quarters as before and in half again into eighths. Cut a small notch at the folds. Open up and line the paper, notched side up, under the equator pins. Adjust the pins to match the notches. You will now have eight evenly-spaced pins around the midpoint of the ball.

DIVISIONS

Cut a length of metallic gold yarn, four and a half times the circumference of the ball. Thread this into the darning needle and push the needle into the ball about 3cm (1¼in) away from the north pole. Bring the point of the needle out just behind the north pole pin, pulling the thread gently until the end slips under the surface. Keeping the thread quite taut as you wrap, wind the thread around the ball past the equator pins and the south pole pin and back up around the other side, past the equator pins and return to the north pole, forming a complete circle.

MATERIALS

- 8cm (3¼in) polystyrene ball
- 250m reel of green sewing cotton
- 1 ball of Peter Pan Gold Fingering (gold metallic knitting yarn), or 1 reel Kreinik No 8 or No 16 braid, gold
- DMC Perlé No 5: one skein each of Red (817), Yellow (742), and White
- 1cm (³⁄₈in) wide strip of paper, longer than the circumference of the ball
- Pins with different coloured heads (berry pins)
- 50cm (½yd) red cord
- 25g ball of green knitting yarn, up to 5-ply
- Darning needle

Note: Use a differnt colour pin to mark the north pole.

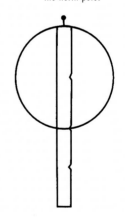

Measuring North and South Poles

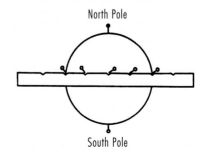

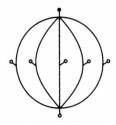

Starter pin

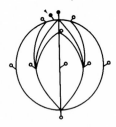

Division lines and equator pins

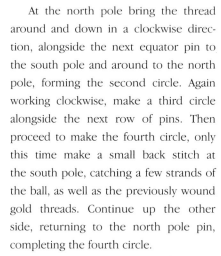

1. *Using red Perlé, repeat the zigzag pattern for three rows.*

2. *Stitching the gold stars.*

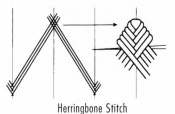

Herringbone Stitch

At the north pole bring the thread around and down in a clockwise direction, alongside the next equator pin to the south pole and around to the north pole, forming the second circle. Again working clockwise, make a third circle alongside the next row of pins. Then proceed to make the fourth circle, only this time make a small back stitch at the south pole, catching a few strands of the ball, as well as the previously wound gold threads. Continue up the other side, returning to the north pole pin, completing the fourth circle.

Secure the top threads with several small stitches and finish by pushing the needle down through the surface and up about 3cm (1¼in) away, trimming any excess thread. Use the back of the needle to push the thread end into the ball's surface. The ball is now marked into eight divisions by the four circles. Keep all pins in place.

EMBROIDERING THE BALL

❖

In the 'Dancing Diamonds' design, threads are worked around the ball in a zigzag pattern using herringbone

stitch. By turning the ball and stitching one colour at a time on opposite hemispheres, an interesting interlocking effect of threads is achieved, creating four diamonds around the equator.

Hold the ball so that the north pole is facing up. With a tape measure and pin, mark 1cm (⅜in) from the north pole on every second gold thread division line. Cut the DMC Perlé threads into 1m (1⅛yd) lengths.

BEGINNING THE WHITE ZIGZAG
Starting with white thread, enter the needle into the ball about 3cm (1¼in) below where one of the pins was just placed. Take the needle under the surface and out just above the pin and to the left of the gold line. Mark the starting point with a different coloured pin, and note its colour. Bring the thread down, moving to the right. Make a small herringbone stitch, right to left, at the next division line just under the equator pin, catching a few strands of the ball's surface. Moving to the right, take the thread up and make a small herringbone stitch at the next division line above the 1cm (⅜in) pin below the north pole.

Continue in this zigzag pattern all around the ball. When you reach the starting point (indicated by the starter pin) make a stitch from right to left,

Northern and southern hemisphere diamonds

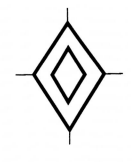

Outlining equator diamonds in red

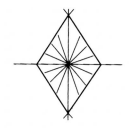

Filling diamonds with star design

bringing the needle just under the first completed row. Do not pull the thread too tightly. You may now remove all the 1cm (³⁄₈in) marker pins except for the starter pin. All other pins remain in place.

Moving to the right, bring the thread directly below the first white row. Make a small stitch, right to left, about 2mm (less than ⅛in) under the previous stitch at the equator. Moving to the right, keep the white thread under the first row. Make another stitch, right to left, just below and over the previous one at the 1cm (³⁄₈in) point. The stitch you have just created should be slightly wider than the top one.

The stitches near the poles will gradually become wider (in a downward direction) as more rows are worked creating a diamond shape. Keep the stitches close together, one underneath the other as more rows are worked. Take care not to pull the stitches too tightly. Always keep the threads below those previously worked. Continue this sequence around the ball until five rows of white are completed. Take the thread under the surface of the ball and trim the excess.

COMPLETING THE WHITE ZIGZAG IN THE SOUTHERN HEMISPHERE

Turn the ball so the south pole is facing upwards. Place pins 1cm (³⁄₈in) from the south pole on the same division lines as before, including a starter pin. Repeat five rows of white in the same zigzag pattern,

beginning at the division line marked with the starter pin. At the equator, the white thread will overlap the ones previously worked around the northern hemisphere. Around the equator you will see four small diamonds emerging. Keep 2mm (less than ⅛in) between stitches at the diamond points.

The equator pins at the diamond centres (only) may be removed after the first row of stitching has been completed right around the southern hemisphere.

STITCHING THE RED AND YELLOW THREAD

Turn the ball so the north pole is facing up and thread the needle with red Perlé. Starting to the left and below the white row on the division line that has the starter pin, repeat the zigzag pattern for three rows (see Step 1). Repeat this step on the southern-hemisphere side.

With yellow Perlé, repeat the zigzag pattern for five rows, first around the northern hemisphere and then around the southern hemisphere.

MARKING THE EQUATOR

Thread a length of metallic gold thread, one and a half times the circumference of the ball. Insert the needle into the ball under one of the equator diamonds and follow the remaining pins around the equator, passing underneath the diamonds. Remove the equator pins.

OUTLINING THE DIAMONDS

Now outline each equator diamond with three rows of red thread. Do this by making a small herringbone stitch at the equator and at the gold division lines at the four points of the diamond.

COMPLETING THE GOLD STARS

With metallic gold thread, make long stitches to create a star effect in the spaces between the equator diamonds (see Step 2).

FINISHING

Make a tassel, 10cm (4in) long with the gold metallic thread and sew it to the south pole. Make a hanging loop using the metallic thread at the north pole. Tie a bow in red cord at the base of the loop and stitch it to the ball.

Felted Mouse

Felt is a versatile, enduring fabric made from wool fleece that is neither spun nor woven. Once you understand the technique of felt-making, the possibilities for creating beautiful garments and craftworks are unlimited. Our felted pincushion is an ideal first project.

FELTING
THE FLEECE

Separate the sliver of fleece into five equal parts and put aside a small amount of fleece for the tail. Take one section of the sliver and wind it around two fingers as if winding a ball of wool. Using one sliver at a time, continue winding the fleece into a ball until it reaches the desired size — approximately 30g (1oz) in weight. Remember that the fleece will have shrunk to about one-third of its original size by the time the felting process is completed. Place the ball into the stocking leg and secure with a knot.

To start the felting process, soak the ball in hot water until it is saturated and swollen. Now place the ball into the washing machine with your regular laundry and washing powder and leave in the washing cycle for three to four minutes only (see Step 1). By this time the fleece fibres will have started to come through the stocking (see Step 2). Remove the ball, squeeze out the excess

Instead of turning your felted ball into a mouse, it can be used to make this elegant pincushion. Omit the ears, tail and face and mount your pincushion on an attractive wood base.

water and gently remove it from the stocking. If the ball has been left in the washing cycle for more than three or four minutes, it will be difficult to extract from the stocking.

Put the ball back into the stocking and place it back in the machine until the cycle has finished. This completes the felting process (see Step 3).

FINISHED SIZE

- Approximately 25cm (10in) in circumference, 10cm (4in) long tail

MATERIALS

- 40g (1½oz) white combed fleece
- Leg from an old stocking
- Appleton's Tapestry Wool: White, Pale Pink, Med. Pink, Dark Pink, Pale Green, Med. Green
- No 9 crewel embroidery needle
- Scissors
- Cotton thread and needle (to sew pearls, attach tail and a ribbon bow)
- Small seed pearls
- No 8 Perlé cotton, black
- Pair of small moveable eyes with shanks
- Square of cream craft felt (for ears)
- Fishing line or clear nylon thread for whiskers
- Craft knife
- Soapy water
- Scrap of satin ribbon

1. *Wind 30g (1oz) of wool sliver into a ball and secure it in a stocking. Thoroughly soak the ball in hot water and then place it in the washing machine with your normal wash.*

2. *Remove the ball after three or four minutes by which time the fleece fibres will have started to come through the stocking.*

 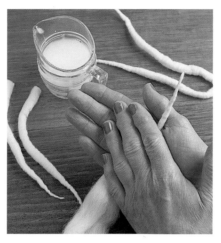 

3. *Gently remove the partially felted ball from the stocking to release the fibres and then return the ball to the stocking. Put it back in the washing machine until the end of the cycle.*

4. *To make the tail, take a small length of the wool sliver and wet it thoroughly in soapy water. Roll it between your hands until the fleece has felted together.*

5. *Make a hole in the back of the mouse's body with a craft knife to attach the tail.*

Take the ball out of the machine and remove the stocking. Roll the ball in your hands for five minutes to firm it up. The more it is rolled, the firmer it will be.

FORMING THE MOUSE

While the ball is still wet, press it into a mouse shape, pinching in at one end to form a nose. Allow to dry completely.

TAIL

To make the tail, thoroughly wet a short length of wool sliver in soapy water. Roll it between your hands until the fleece has felted together (see Step 4). Allow to dry. With a pair of scissors or a craft knife, make a hole in the back of the mouse and attach the tail by stitching securely (see Step 5).

EARS

Using the pattern supplied, cut four ears from commercial felt. With the crewel needle threaded with pale pink wool, make three lazy daisy stitches in the inner ear. Pin two ear pieces together and blanket stitch around the outer edge using white embroidery wool. Sew on each ear, gathering the base of the ear slightly as you sew. It is best to sew the ears in place before positioning the eyes.

FACIAL FEATURES

Embroider the nose in black Perlé cotton using six straight stitches placed close together, then attach the eyes.

Cut 10cm (4in) lengths of fishing line for the whiskers and sew in place. Tie a knot close to the face so the whiskers cannot be detached.

Embroidery Stitch Diagram

Mouse Ear Pattern

WOOL ROSES

Work each layer of the rose using a different shade of wool, starting with the darkest shade of pink for the centre and working out to the pale pink outer petals.

1. Work five, 4mm (¹⁄₈in) satin stitches close together, then work seven satin stitches close together over the previous stitches. Make these stitches 12mm (¹⁄₂in) long, extending them beyond the first layer on one side only.

2. Bring your needle up at any corner and take a stitch diagonally across the corner. Take the next stitch back to the same corner, but a little further over, creating a slight angle on your stitch. These two stitches are embroidered in one movement (push the needle from one point to another in one motion).

   At the third stitch, go straight down and turn the fabric anti-clockwise to work three stitches over the next corner. Stitch all corners in this manner. This completes the second layer of the rose.

3. To complete the rose and make it round, stem stitch in an anti-clockwise direction with the wool on top of the rose and keeping the stitches 12mm (¹⁄₂in) long. Work two stitches past where you began.

4. In the darkest colour, work one narrow fly stitch. Add a straight stitch in the medium colour to fit snugly in the V of the fly stitch, extending it slightly beyond the points of the fly stitch.

5. Change to the lightest colour and embroider a fly stitch around the outside of the first one. Work a third fly stitch in light green around the other two, with the holding stitch of the fly stitch forming the stem of the bud. Still using light green, embroider two stitches in a V-shape at the top of the bud.

EMBROIDERY

The embroidery consists of one large wool rose, three stems with rosebuds and leaves, five fern fronds and nine cream pearls. Following the Embroidery Stitch Diagram on page 102, work the design in the recommended colours, or the colours of your choosing. For the rose and rosebuds, follow the step-by-step photograph and instructions to the right.

FERN FRONDS

Take the green tapestry wool and stitch a series of fly stitches to create the fern fronds. You may wish to stitch the fern fronds in two different shades of green.

PEARLS

To add the final touch of the small seed pearls, use the cotton thread and sewing needle. Attach them into position, by sewing them on as indicated on the Embroidery Stitch Diagram supplied on page 102.

FINISHING

To add the finishing touch to your country, felted mouse, sew a small length of the satin ribbon in a bow at the base of the tail. By doing this, you will also cover any stitches left when attaching the tail.

Fancy Glass

Most people have an embossed glass plate or a bowl in their cupboards. Bring it out and give it a new lease on life with this simple, innovative method of glass decoration. No pattern is needed as the design is already stamped into the glass.

GENERAL TIPS FOR REVERSE GLASS-PAINTING

The term 'reverse glass-painting' refers not only to the fact that you are working on the reverse side of the glass, but also to the fact that you paint in the reverse order to normal painting.

Choose glass items with attractive stamped floral patterns. We found tulip and hydrangea designs at inexpensive prices at the local variety store. With our hydrangea design we painted the entire back of the platter. With the tulips, only the embossed sections were painted. Decide which effect would best suit your plate.

As you go, check your progress by constantly turning the plate to the right side. It's a bit disconcerting at first, but you will soon get the hang of it. Don't worry if the back looks messy (it will be tidied up at the end). If you make a mistake or don't like the effect, remove that section with a damp cotton bud and start again.

PREPARATION

Turn the glassware upside down. Clean the surface with a cloth. Using a large flat brush or a sponge brush, paint a coat of Glass and Tile Primer over the reverse side. If you are painting the embossed motifs only, apply the primer only to those areas. The primer provides a good base for the paint. It is clear and looks like water. Allow it to dry before proceeding.

MATERIALS

- Clear stamped glass bowl or platter
- Jo Sonja's Glass and Tile Primer
- Jo Sonja's Glass and Tile Painting Medium
- Cotton buds
- Cloth
- Water-based polyurethane satin varnish
- Large flat brush or sponge brush for priming
- No 2 or 3 round brush

TULIP PLATTER

- Jo Sonja's Artists' Acrylics: Turners Yellow, Warm White, Rose Pink, Burnt Sienna, Moss Green, Pine Green

HYDRANGEA PLATTER

- Jo Sonja's Artists' Acrylics: Moss Green, Warm White, Pine Green, Turners Yellow, Smoked Pearl, Napthol Red Light, Dioxazine Purple, Pthalo Blue

The design is painted onto the reverse side of the glass.

Painting is done in the reverse order, with the details painted first and the background last.

FINISHING

Leave the paint to dry for a few days. No heat-setting is required if you have used primer. Then varnish the reverse side with a couple of coats of water-based polyurethane satin varnish to give it extra protection. Put the piece away for a few weeks to allow the painted surface to harden and cure.

MAINTENANCE

Care for your reverse-painted glass by gently hand-washing it in warm water. It is not advised to rub or immerse the piece in water. Pat dry. Never place hand-painted pieces in a dishwasher. For a gift, place a card inside, to indicate the maintenance instructions.

PAINTING THE DESIGN

For all stages use a No 2 or 3 round brush, but if there are any narrow areas like the stems, you may prefer a finer brush. Mix each colour with Glass and Tile Painting Medium in about equal parts. Brush-mix the Glass and Tile Painting Medium into the paint as you go. Allow each layer or stage to dry before applying the next, or the colour will lift.

Do any fine line work or details like dot centres and stamens first. Then paint the highlights, starting with the brightest. Apply the paint thinly and smoothly, just skimming the surface. Do not add water to the paint. Ensure the edges of each highlight are feathered off rather than ending with a line. When dry, apply some further highlights over the top and extend out beyond the first area you painted. Don't make the highlights so large they will engulf the whole flower. Next paint the shadows, again feathering the edges so there are no harsh lines. Remember to leave space for the base colour.

Finally do the base-painting. This involves colouring-in all the gaps on the flower or leaves with the base colour and painting over the entire motif. Two to three coats will be necessary, but allow each coat to dry thoroughly before applying the next. This final step makes the painted areas opaque and tidies up the underside of the item.

At the end hold your glass up to the light to check whether there are any tiny gaps where you have not painted, and fill them in.

COLOURS FOR THE TULIP PLATTER

TULIPS

Paint the stamens Turners Yellow. Paint small highlights of Warm White plus a little Rose Pink on the centres of the petals. Add further larger highlights over the top and beyond with a mixture of equal parts Rose Pink and Warm White. Paint a few shadows with a mix of Rose Pink and Burnt Sienna. Colour in the rest of the tulip with Rose Pink.

LEAVES AND STEMS

Mix equal quantities of Moss Green and Warm White and paint some highlights on the widest areas of the leaves. Add some further highlights of Moss Green. Fill in the rest of the leaves and stems

Painted glassware makes a wonderful gift if you can bear to part with it. If you don't already own a clear embossed glass bowl or platter, they can be bought very cheaply from discount stores. Even items intended for serving food can be painted on because you work on the reverse side.

with a mix of equal parts of Moss Green and Pine Green.

Leave the paint to dry for several days then follow the finishing instructions set out above.

COLOURS FOR THE HYDRANGEA PLATTER

PINK HYDRANGEAS

Mix two parts Smoked Pearl with one part Napthol Red and paint some pink flowers. Add a touch of Turners Yellow

to the mix and paint some pinkish-apricot flowers. Finally, paint some lighter pink flowers by adding Warm White to the mix. Centres are Turners Yellow, outlined with pink.

PURPLE HYDRANGEAS

Mix two parts Smoked Pearl to one part Dioxazine Purple and paint the flowers. Add Warm White to the mix to create some lighter flowers. Shade around the centre of some of the flowers with extra Dioxazine Purple. Centres are Turners Yellow, partly outlined in Napthol Red.

BLUE HYDRANGEAS

Use variations of Smoked Pearl and Pthalo Blue to make some flowers darker and others lighter. Centres are Turners Yellow, partly outlined in Napthol Red.

LEAVES

Use Pine Green and mix in a little Turners Yellow here and there for variety.

BACKGROUND

Fill in the background with a mix of two parts Smoked Pearl to one of Pine Green. You will need several coats. Leave the paint to dry for several days then follow the finishing instructions above.

Full bloom

Flowers are a popular motif in country crafts. They suggest beauty and simplicity, fresh air and sunlight. They remind us of the abundance of old-fashioned cottage gardens. Some of these projects could be tackled by a beginner, but most are suited to the experienced craftsperson.

Gold Lace and Pansies

Delicate pansies have been perfectly matched with this fine lace pattern to create a powder box reminiscent of the Victorian era. Imitation gold leaf work on the interior completes the opulent design. You'll need a neat and steady hand and some experience of folk art techniques.

PREPARATION

Sand the entire bowl, inside and out, and remove any dust. Apply several coats of black gesso allowing it to dry thoroughly before applying the next coat. Sand between coats and continue until you have a smooth finish. The inside needs to be as smooth as possible for applying the gold leaf.

After sanding the surface, apply several coats of bole to the inside of both the bottom and the lid. Allow six to ten hours before proceeding with the gold leaf.

APPLYING THE GOLD LEAF

Do not to let the Dutch metal (imitation gold leaf) come in contact with your skin, as the oils from your skin will cause it to tarnish and you may see finger marks after varnishing.

Before cutting the leaf, dust your hands with talc. Hold the leaf between the tissue paper packaging and cut some long narrow strips for the sides. Then cut the remainder into larger squares to fit the inside surfaces. Set the leaf aside.

As size dries quickly, apply it to a small area at a time, starting with the inside lid of the box and then moving on to the inside surface of the bottom. Using a 20mm (3/4in) flat brush, apply the size thinly and smoothly over the bole, being careful not to overwork the surface or it will bead. Wash your brush thoroughly in water when finished.

To gauge when the size is ready for the gold leaf, wait five to seven minutes then test the tackiness using your knuckles. When it feels like sticky tape, it is ready for the leaf to be applied. The working time of the size varies from fifteen to forty minutes depending on the temperature. If you are unsure about the working time, work half the lid at a time.

Dust your hands again with talc then, using the tweezers, remove the tissue paper and pick up a piece of leaf and lay it onto your sized area. Flatten the leaf with the bristle brush to remove any size that may have been picked up. Apply the next piece of leaf, overlapping the first piece slightly, and flatten it down with the bristle brush as before. Follow this procedure until you have covered the entire area. If you apply the leaf systematically the result will be much better.

When the area has been gilded, use a dry bristle brush to dust off any loose leaf pieces. Do this over a clean piece of paper and retain these flakes, known as 'skew', to use later on the outside of the lid. Then wipe the entire area with a soft cloth. If you are not happy with the result so far, you may re-gild spots or the entire surface using the same process.

Allow the leaf to sit for approximately four to six hours and then use a flat brush to apply a thin coat of Aging Glaze. Wait four hours and apply one coat of Leaf Varnish — this prevents further aging through oxidation and protects the surface from handling.

PREPARING THE OUTSIDE OF THE LID

Lightly mark the centre of the lid with a pencil. Set the compass to a radius of 32mm (1 1/4in) and lightly draw in the circle marked 1 on the Painting Guide. Then draw in circles 2 and 3 by setting the compass to 36mm (1 1/2in) and 44mm (1 3/4in).

Apply a thin coat of size to the entire area inside the inner circle. Allow the size to become tacky then, using the stencil brush, mash the skew until it is fine. Use the stencil brush to flick the fine pieces of

FINISHED SIZE

- 14cm (5 1/2in) bowl

MATERIALS

- 14cm (5 1/2in) powder bowl
- Jo Sonja's Artists' Acrylics: Rich Gold, Green Oxide, Teal, Smoked Pearl, Turners Yellow, Raw Sienna, Fawn, Diox Purple, Yellow Light, Carbon Black, Warm White, Storm Blue, Burnt Umber.
- 1 or 2 packets Dutch metal leaf
- Bole
- Size
- Aging Glaze
- Leaf Varnish
- Basecoating brush
- 20mm (3/4in) flat brush for sizing
- No 2 and No 3 Raphael 8404 brush
- Varnishing brush
- Stiff stencil brush
- 12mm (1/2in) bristle brush
- Liner brush (optional)
- Eraser
- White transfer paper
- Fine-tipped pen
- Compass
- Pencil
- Talc
- Scissors
- Fine sandpaper
- Tracing paper
- Stylus
- Black gesso
- Soft lint-free cloth
- Acrylic gloss and satin varnish
- Jo Sonja's Retarder & Antiquing Medium
- Tweezers

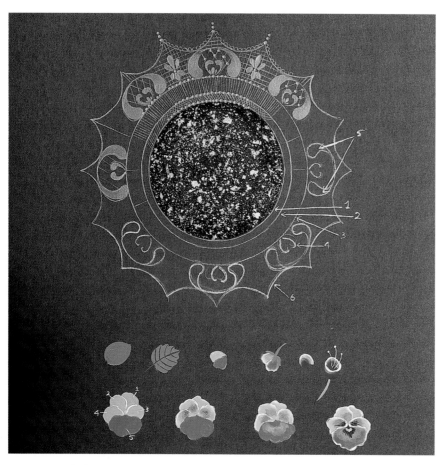

Painting Guide for the lid design.

PAINTING THE LACE

Squeeze some Rich Gold onto the palette. For smooth flowing lines, dress the liner or No 3 brush in flow medium and wipe it into the Rich Gold, flattening it on the palette. Start by painting in the three circles (1, 2 and 3 on the Painting Guide). Next paint the outside line (marked 6). You are now ready to begin the detail on the lace.

Start with the fine crisscross lines in the band surrounding the centre. Paint in the lines in one direction first, continually moving the lid around to keep the correct slope. Change the painting direction and continue in the same way until the band is completed. On the next band paint fine lines all pointing to the centre. Work these lines a sections at a time. Paint the fine lines inside the large commas and in the outer section as shown on the pattern. Use the stylus for the dots on the circles and outside the outer line.

Finally, paint in the comma strokes marked 4 on the Guide and then the commas marked 5. The small foot on the base of the bowl is also painted gold.

leaf skew onto the sized area. Then, with the stencil brush, scrumble over the gold skew to flatten and spread it. Apply one coat of Leaf Varnish being careful to stay strictly within the circle. Allow it to dry (approximately thirty minutes) and sand lightly.

Using a light pencil, divide the circles into sixteen even sections. Trace the pattern onto tracing paper, using a fine-tipped pen for the pansy design. Because the lid of this bowl is curved and the pattern is on a flat piece of paper, you may need to clip the edge of the pattern. Make sure the pattern is centred on the lid then, using white transfer paper and a stylus, transfer only the commas and the outside line of the design (marked 4, 5 and 6 on the Painting Guide) at this stage. The detailed lines of the lace are painted freehand and the pansy design is transferred later.

PAINTING THE PANSIES

Transfer only the pansies and the leaves onto the centre of the lid at this stage. Using the No 2 brush, block in the pansies with a thin coat of Smoked Pearl, following the shape of the petals. Block the leaves in with Green Oxide. Allow to dry.

Apply another coat to the leaves using the tip of the brush to create the small scalloped edges. When dry add fine veins with the liner brush using Teal. Apply another coat of Smoked Pearl to the pansies so they are opaque and smooth. If necessary, use your pencil to mark in the divisions of the petals.

All the pansies are painted using the same method, varying only in the use of colour as outlined below. Use the Painting Guide and photograph of the finished box as guides.

PANSY NO 1

Using Fawn and a touch of Diox Purple, block in the back petal (marked 1 on the Guide) — it may require two coats. Side-load the tip of your brush with a small amount of Warm White and lightly highlight the edge of the petal. Proceed to the petal marked 2 on the Guide and block in with a Fawn and Diox Purple mix, then highlight the edge of the petal. Petals 3 and 4 are painted in the same manner. The front petal (5 on the Guide) is blocked in with Diox Purple with a small amount of fawn added. Petals 2, 3 and 4 have a light watery wash of the front petal colour and the front petal has a watery wash of the back petal colour. Allow to dry. Then side-load your brush with Warm White and paint in the highlight around the edge of the front petal and use Carbon Black to mark fine lines from the centre of petals 3, 4 and 5 about one third of the way along each one. When the black has dried, paint fine lines using Yellow Light around the centre of the front petal. The yellow should not cover the black entirely. Pick up Warm White with the tip of your round brush and add a small comma either side of the centre on the front petal. Add a little extra white where needed on the edge of some petals. Using these same colours and the same method, paint the two buds either side of pansy No 2.

PANSY NO 2

Following the method for Pansy No 1, block in with Turners Yellow, shade the division between petals with Raw Sienna. Highlight the edges of all petals with Warm White and paint the face of the pansy and the third bud with Carbon Black and Yellow Light.

LID TEMPLATE

115%

PANSY NO 3

This pansy is painted using a combination of the colours of the other two flowers. The back two petals are painted in the purple mix and lightly highlighted first with the fawn mix and then edged in Warm White. The three front petals are painted with Turners Yellow, Raw Sienna and Warm White.

OTHER FLORA

Paint the leaves and stems of the three pansy buds in Green Oxide, using the No 2 brush.

Now draw or trace the filler flowers onto the bowl. Load the No 2 brush with Storm Blue and add a side-load blend of Warm White. The flowers are tiny, so be careful not to overload the brush. Paint the rear of the little flowers first using a half swivel stroke. The front stroke joins on to the edge and curves down then back up to join at the other side. Paint

three fine white stamens from each centre and add a tiny white dot to the ends. Lighten some Green Oxide with a little Warm White and paint a stem on each filler flower. Allow the paint to dry thoroughly and erase any tracing or drawing lines.

FINISHING

Once the paint has cured (this normally takes 1–2 days) use a very light application of Jo Sonja's Retarder and Antiquing Medium with Burnt Umber to antique the centre area of your lid.

When dry, varnish the bowl. Give the inside gilded areas two coats of gloss varnish and the outside three coats of satin varnish, lightly sand the surface after the second coat to achieve a smooth finish.

Fuchsia and Violets

*These delicate florals on organza are outlined in dimensional paint
and then embroidered with simple stitches. The finished images,
mounted in box frames, cast a shadow on the back mount
which creates an intriguing extra dimension.*

PREPARATION

If using a frame, stretch the organza as firmly as possible and staple it to the edges. If using an embroidery hoop, stretch the fabric and fasten it in the hoop permanently. The finished work should not be taken out of the frame or hoop, but mounted 'as is' in an attractive display frame.

Trace the design outline from the pattern on page 117 onto the stretched organza using a sharp 2B pencil.

PAINTING THE DESIGN

Elevate the organza by placing a pencil or pen under one side of the frame or embroidery hoop. This prevents the paint from bleeding under the organza.

Apply the black Colourpoint paint finely and evenly over the design lines. Practise first on a scrap of fabric or paper until you feel confident. Paint only over the solid lines of the design, not the dotted ones. Dry the paint by using a hair dryer on both the front and the back of the organza.

EMBROIDERING THE VIOLETS

Work the flowers in satin stitch within the confines of the paint. Satin stitching is easy when working with organza as the underlying stitch shows through thus hiding any gaps in the surface stitching.

Work the orange centre of the flower with three straight stitches and a French knot in the middle of the flower. Work five or six Silver straight stitches fanning out from the centre of the flower. Work

the stems in whipped running stitch through the painted stems.

Use long straight stitches to embroider the veins of the leaves and couch these stitches in place. Fill in between the veins with long stitches in Dark Green, fanning out from the veins as indicated by the dotted lines on the Stitching Guide (page 117). Straight stitch over the painted outline, alternating light and dark threads. Increase the length of the stitch towards the tips of the leaves.

Finish off the posy of violets with a small bow of silk ribbon. With a tapestry needle, pierce the organza where indicated on the Guide on page 117. Thread the ribbon into the needle and bring one end up through the organza. Repeat with other end of the ribbon. Tie a bow and catch the loops to the organza. Take the ends of the ribbon back through the organza and catch in place.

EMBROIDERING THE FUCHSIA

All embroidery is worked with a single strand of thread. Refer to the Stitching and Colour Guide on page 117 and to the detail photograph on page 116.

Embroider the calyx (outer petals) of the fuchsia with long, fanned-out straight stitches in Coral Pink. Work the corolla (inner petals) in long, fanned out straight

FINISHED SIZE

- 15cm (6in) square

MATERIALS

- 25cm (10in) square of organza

- 2 x approximately 15cm (6in) square frames or an approximately 15cm (6in) in diameter embroidery hoop

- 2 Staples and gun to penetrate the frame

- 2 Tubes of Tulip Colourpoint paint, black

- 2B pencil

- 2 No 9 quilting needle

VIOLETS

- Madeira Silk embroidery thread: two skeins each of Light Green (1409), Dark Green (1407), Pink Violet (0713), Orange (0206)

- Madeira Decora: two skeins each of Plum Violet (1433), Royal Violet (1522)

- Madeira Metallic thread: two skeins of Silver (9803/3010)

- 23mm (1in) silk ribbon for bow on violets

FUCHSIA

- Madeira Silk embroidery thread: one skein each of Coral Pink (0506), Dark Green (1407), Light Green (1408), Dark Mauve (0711), Light Mauve (0801)

- Madeira Decora: one skein of Purple (1433)

Detail photograph of the embroidered violets.

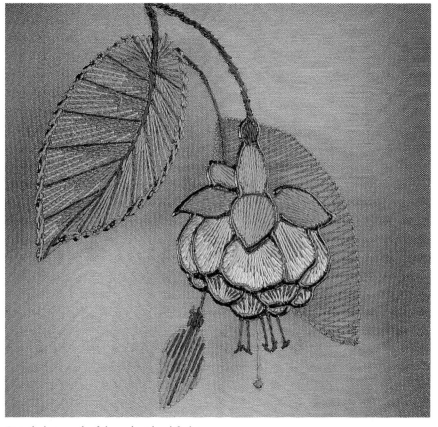

Detail photograph of the embroidered fuchsias.

stitches also, but in Dark Mauve. High-light the corolla with Light Mauve long and short straight stitches, between the Dark Mauve. Shade the corolla with small straight stitches in Purple between the Dark Mauve.

Work the pistil in whipped running stitch in Coral Pink, finishing with a French knot (4 wraps). The stamens are worked the same way, but in Purple, and with a straight stitch on a slant at the end. Couch the painted stems in Purple.

Stitch the bud of the fuchsia with long straight stitches, alternating the Coral Pink and the Purple.

The leaf behind the flower is worked in shadow stitch in Dark Green. For the leaf in the foreground, use Purple to work the centre vein in whipped running stitch and the rest of the veins in long straight stitches. Fill in between the veins with long, fanned-out straight stitches in Dark Green. Highlight the leaf with long straight stitches in Light Green. Work straight stitches in dark green over the leaf outline, increasing the length of the stitch towards the tip of the leaf.

FRAMING

Your finished work should be framed so that the glass does not touch the embroidery and so that there is also space behind the fabric. The backing should be a light colour to show the shadow of the embroidery. It would be best to have your embroidery framed professionally.

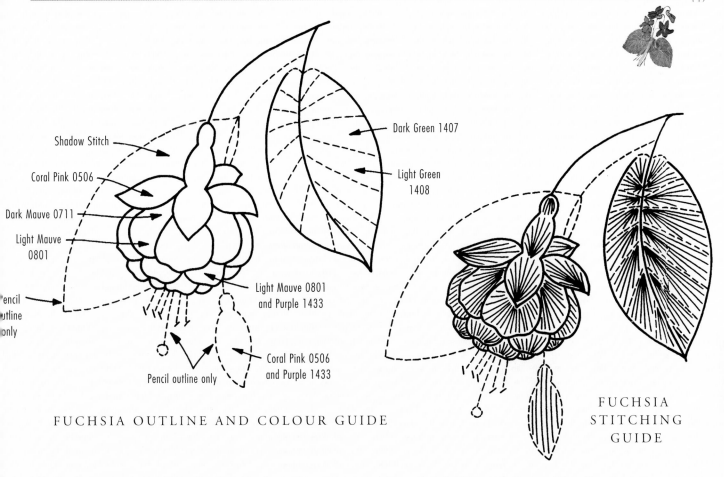

Shadow Stitch

Coral Pink 0506

Dark Mauve 0711

Light Mauve 0801

Pencil outline only

Light Mauve 0801 and Purple 1433

Pencil outline only

Coral Pink 0506 and Purple 1433

Dark Green 1407

Light Green 1408

FUCHSIA OUTLINE AND COLOUR GUIDE

FUCHSIA STITCHING GUIDE

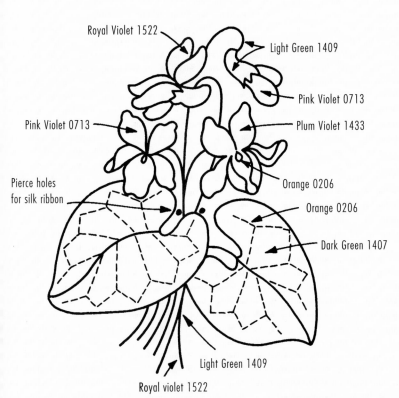

Royal Violet 1522

Light Green 1409

Pink Violet 0713

Plum Violet 1433

Pink Violet 0713

Orange 0206

Pierce holes for silk ribbon

Orange 0206

Dark Green 1407

Light Green 1409

Royal violet 1522

VIOLETS OUTLINE AND COLOUR GUIDE

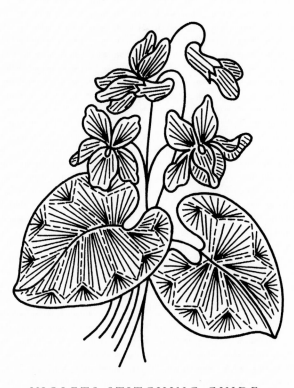

VIOLETS STITCHING GUIDE

SS

Table of Tuscan Lemons

Lemons and blossoms transform a plain, round table of any size into a work of art. This stunning design is easy for even relative beginners to paint and will breathe new life into an old garden table, or give a unique finish to a new one.

PAINTING THE DESIGN

❖

Use the Russian round brush for all basic brushstrokes and the liner brush for all fine detailing.

LEMONS

Dabble Canary over the lemons, leaving plenty of white showing through as highlights. To create depth, add a little Sierra Gold to the ends and border outline of the lemons.

LEAVES

Paint about half the leaves Grasshopper, varying the depth of colour to give a two-tone effect. Side-load and brush around the leaves' edges and centre veins. Brushstroke in the leaves over the yellow edge tiles. Paint the remaining leaves with Juniper, again varying the depth and colour.

PREPARATION

❖

Sand away any ridges or blemishes on the tabletop. Wipe off any dust and coat once with the White Bisq Stain or twice with the White Spray Stain.

Trace the design from the pattern on page 121 onto tracing paper, if necessary enlarging or reducing the size of it to fit your tabletop. Centre the pattern on the tabletop and attach it to the table with masking tape. Slip the graphite paper under the tracing paper and gently trace the pattern with the pencil.

FINISHED SIZE

- Designed to fit any small, cafe-style round table

MATERIALS

- 47cm (19in) diameter Bisque tabletop
- Wrought-iron legs
- Fine sandpaper
- Lint-free cloth
- Tracing paper
- Saral or graphite paper and pencil
- Masking tape
- Isopropyl alcohol
- Wool sponge
- Turntable (optional)
- Russian round small brush
- 10/0 fine liner brush
- Soft, goat-hair fan brush
- Paper towelling
- Duncan Sheer Strokes paint: Canary, Sierra Gold, Grasshopper, Juniper, Pecan, Coal, Plantation, Sapphire
- Paint palette
- White Bisq Stain or White Spray Stain
- Bisq-Seal Brush-On Gloss Varnish
- Epoxy glue (two-pack)

NOTE

Most of the materials above apply to painting the design on a bisque tabletop. However, by adapting the sealing, painting and finishing mediums to suit the material from which the tabletop is made (for example wood or enamel), the design can be applied to any round table. It can also be adapted to a tabletop of any size — just enlarge or reduce your pattern to fit.

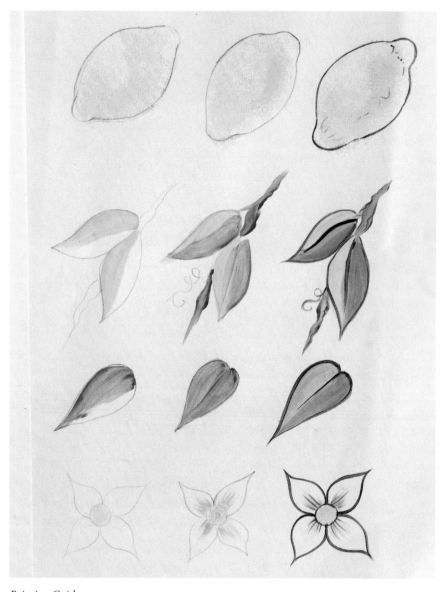

Painting Guide

BORDERS

Using the photograph as a guide, paint in the Sierra Gold band around the outside of the design. With a damp brush, add a band of Coal outside the Sierra Gold edge. It is easier to complete this process using a turntable, but it can be done freehand. Fill in the four edge tiles with Canary and add Coal edging bands to both sides of each tile.

Squeeze equal quantities of Plantation Grasshopper, and Juniper onto your palette and dip different parts of the sponge into the different colours. Press the sponge onto the palette to get rid of any excess paint and dab it over the remaining edge band of the table to create a mottled look. Allow to dry thoroughly.

Thin Sapphire with water, and edge the Coal bands, brushing out a section at a time and immediately dabbing softly with the sponge dipped in isopropyl. This removes and repels the Sapphire, exposing the colours underneath. Do not brush-out the colour too far ahead, as the technique is not as effective when the colour has dried. Dip in water and side-load the round brush with Sapphire. Shade in a shadow around the inside edges of the Sierra Gold band and along the inside edges of the lemon and blossom design.

BLOSSOM

Brush Juniper out from the centre of the flowers. Squeeze some Canary onto the palette and allow it to thicken. Wash the brush and dry it on a paper towel or a cloth. Flatten the bush into the thickened paint, wipe most of the paint off the brush onto a paper towel and lightly brush over the centres of all flowers.

BRANCHES

Load the brush with Pecan, side-dip in the Canary and brush with smooth flowing lines over all the branches.

DETAILING

Thin the Coal with a little water. Using the fine liner brush, outline and detail all design lines and the bands.

FINISHING

Leave to dry for twenty-four hours. With the soft, goat-hair fan brush, apply several coats of Bisq-Seal and allow to dry well. Secure the top to the legs using the epoxy glue.

TABLE OF TUSCAN LEMONS
Design Outline

133%

Jessica's Dressing Table Set

A personalised brush, comb and mirror set is the perfect gift for someone who appreciates the design and skill involved in a hand-worked item. As the embroidered area is relatively small, this project will appeal to cross-stitchers with limited time to devote to their craft.

MATERIALS

- Brush, comb and mirror set

- 30cm x 25cm (12in x 10in) 14-count ecru diamond Aida cloth

- DMC Stranded Embroidery Cotton: one skein each of Apricot (3341), Light Apricot (3824), Very Light Sportsman Flesh (951), Very Light Golden Yellow (3078), White, Delft (809), Pale Geranium (957), Geranium (956), Dark Forest Green (987), Forest Green (989), Very Light Yellow Green (772)

- No 26 tapestry needle

- Small amount of batting to cover the mirror and brush backs

Detail of the brush cross-stitch.

PREPARATION

Follow the manufacturer's mirror and brush disassembly instructions, then use the card inside as a guide for fabric size. Cut the Aida cloth quite a bit larger than needed and sew small running stitches around the edges to prevent fraying. Fold the fabric horizontally and vertically to find the centre and mark this with a stitch of thread. Photocopy the designs on page 124 to 126, enlarging them if necessary.

STITCHING THE DESIGN

Find and mark the centre of each design on the Stitch Guides. Align the centre point on each pattern with the centre point of the cloth and, following the Stitch Guides and Colour Key, work the design in cross-stitch with two strands of thread.

Once all the cross stitching has been completed, outline the ribbon, flowers, leaves and buds in back stitch using a single thread. Matching the centre point of whatever initial you require with the centre of the design for the mirror back, cross-stitch the letter in Delft then outline it in back stitch using Forest Green.

ASSEMBLING THE SET

Very carefully trim the fabric to size. Cut a piece of batting the same size as the fabric and layer it under the embroidery. Finish with the assembly of the mirror and brush according to the manufacturer's instructions. Care and patience is needed when fitting the acetate covering.

Detail of the mirror cross-stitch.

MIRROR STITCH GUIDE

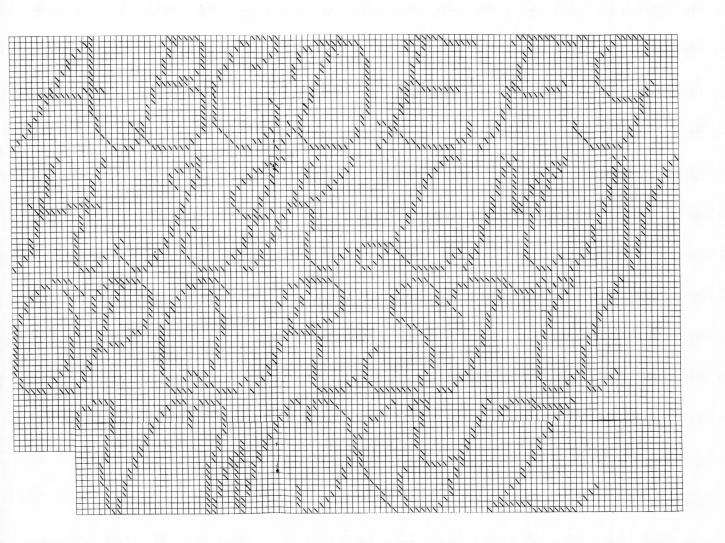

ALPHABET STITCH GUIDE

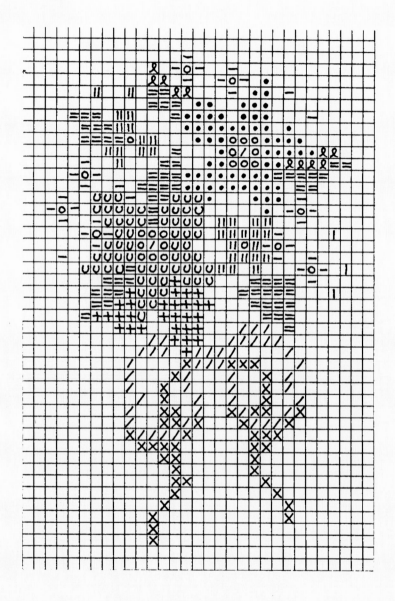

STITCH
COLOUR KEY

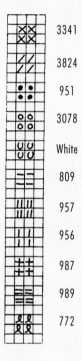

	3341
	3824
	951
	3078
	White
	809
	957
	956
	987
	989
	772

BRUSH STITCH GUIDE

Floral Topiary

Delicate silk flowers, colourful dried foliage and terracotta combine to stunning effect in this attractive topiary arrangement. As the main colour can be changed quite easily while still retaining the background foliage, this arrangement can accommodate any colour scheme to suit any home decor.

FINISHED SIZE

- Approximately 40cm (15¾in)

MATERIALS

- Half a floral oasis block
- 7cm (2¾in) in diameter, floral oasis ball
- 11cm (4⅜in) in diameter, terracotta pot
- 30cm (12in) tree stem
- Moss
- Thin wire
- Ribbon for bow
- Craft glue
- Scissors
- Pliers
- Knife
- Blue gum foliage
- Banksia leaves
- Bleached Chinese puzzle
- White tea tree stems
- Pink ixodia daisies (SA or Ost daisies)
- 12 cream polysilk baby roses
- 12 burgundy polysilk baby roses

Gather and sort your materials before you start.

PREPARATION

Cut the oasis to fit snugly into the pot and glue it into position. Insert the tree stem into the middle of the pot, pushing it firmly into the oasis. Remove the stem and fill the hole with glue, replace the stem, then glue around the base of the stem to hold it in place.

Push the other end of the tree stem into the oasis ball, so that it goes half way through the ball. Remove the stem and fill the hole with glue, then replace the stem. Glue around the stem and ball to secure it. Allow the glue to set.

THE BACKGROUND FOLIAGE

Cut, rather than break, the banksia, gum and tea tree into lengths of 8–10cms (3¼–4ins), as this will give a cleaner end for sticking into the oasis. It is normally not necessary to wire the foliage, but you may wish to lengthen any short pieces or strengthen weak stems by attaching wire. Glue the end of the stems and push them into the oasis, turning the pot as you work to ensure an even distribution of the foliage over the entire ball. Make some stems longer so they stick out of the ball further than others, to give a softer effect and to avoid a cropped look.

THE FLOWERS

Cut the stems of the roses to about 7cm (2¾in) and glue and stick them evenly around the oasis ball, placing first the burgundy and then the cream roses to ensure an even distribution. The roses should be shorter than the foliage.

Cut the bleached Chinese puzzle into short heads and distribute it at intervals around the oasis ball between the roses and the background foliage.

Break off the daisies and mass them together in small bunches, filling any gaps around the ball. Turn the topiary tree around to check for balance and harmony of colour and texture.

FINISHING

Cover the oasis in the pot with moss, securing it in place with a line of glue around the outer edges of the oasis. Bend small pieces of wire in half and push them through the moss and into the oasis.

Finally, create a bow with long ties, attach wire to it and insert it into the topiary close to the stem, so the loops form part of the arrangement and the ribbon hangs down the stem.

CARING FOR THE TOPIARY ARRANGEMENT

Dust the arrangement every so often by blowing softly on it or using a hair dryer on a low setting. Do not use hair spray on the topiary as it will eventually discolour it. Hair spray will also make the arrangement sticky so that it is even harder to remove the dust.

Summer Rose

The muted shading and gentle contrasts of this rose in bloom are achieved by the technique of shadow trapunto, which involves both quilting and shadow stitching. The design is worked on the wrong side of the batiste, so the stitching glows through the sheer fabric.

PREPARATION

Trace or photocopy the Design Outline on page 133 onto a large piece of paper. Mark the centre point of the design, then lay the paper onto a flat surface and secure it with masking tape.

Fold one of the batiste squares into quarters and finger-press to find the centre. Matching the centre of the design with the centre of the fabric, place the fabric over the pattern and secure it with tape. Using a 2B pencil, lightly trace the solid lines of the design onto the fabric. Do not trace the dotted lines yet.

Sandwich the batting between the two layers of fabric, with both batiste pieces facing right-side out. Using long stitches, tack the three layers together in a grid pattern (see Step 1).

STITCHING THE DESIGN

Using one strand of the embroidery cotton (1512) and a quilting needle, stitch around the design using small, even running stitches. After completing this stitching remove the tacking stitches.

On the back of the design, lightly draw the dotted lines shown on the pattern. These lines indicate a colour change across the petals (refer to the design outline on page 133).

Using the Colour Guide on the Design Outline, thread the needle with the correct, coloured wool. Work with a double yarn from the wrong side of the work, drawing the wool between the batting and the top layer of fabric. Insert the needle through the bottom layer and the batting, but do not go through the top layer, when bringing

FINISHED SIZE

- 30cm (12in) square

MATERIALS

- 2 x 30cm (12in) squares of batiste fabric
- 30cm (12in) square of polyester batting, split in half
- 1 skein of Madeira Stranded embroidery Cotton (1512)
- No 10 quilting betweens needle
- No 20 tapestry needle
- DMC tapestry wool: 1 skein each of: Red (7849), Deep Pink (7605), Pale Pink (7132), Orange (7947), Cream (7746), Pale Green (7382), Dark Green (7541), Emerald Green (7911), Deep Yellow (7050), Yellow (7726), Light Blue (7799), Black
- 2B pencil
- Masking tape

1. *First stitch the three layers together using large tacking stiches, then stitch the design lines using small, even running stitches.*

the needle out at the other end of the stitch. Pull the yarn through leaving a tiny tail approximately 2mm (⅛in) at the starting point and cutting the thread close to the fabric at the exit point (see Step 2). Continue stitching and cutting the yarn in this manner, until one section of the rose is full.

Using the point of the needle or your fingers, stroke or pull the yarn back inside the design. Do not try to push the ends in with the needle, but rather use the needle as a hook by inserting it just under the bottom layer of fabric and giving it a twist to pull the tiny ends inside the design.

Continue stitching and drawing in the yarn one section at a time, until the design is completed and all sections are coloured. The yarn should be like long stitches just under the top fabric. Hold your finished work to the light to see if more yarn is necessary. Do not over-stuff, but rather do a little all over then go back and add more if required for colour or dimension.

FRAMING THE DESIGN

When your Summer Rose shadow trapunto work is completed, have your piece professionally framed as shown in the photograph to best show it off. Alternatively, you can use your piece as the centre design for a cushion or to decorate the padded top of a favourite work basket or box.

2. *Remove the tacking lines then thread the needle with wool in the appropriate colour. Draw the double yarn between the batting and the top layer, leaving tiny tails at each end of each stitch.*

SHADOW TRAPUNTO DESIGN OUTLINE

COLOUR GUIDE AND KEY

DMC TAPESTRY WOOL

a = 7849 Red
b = 7605 Deep Pink
c = 7132 Pale Pink
d = 7947 Orange
e = 7746 Cream
f = 7382 Pale Green
g = 7541 Dark Green
h = 7911 Emerald Green
i = 7050 Deep Yellow
j = 7726 Yellow
k = Black
l = 7799 Light Blue

Tulip Planter Box

*Welcome spring, and brighten up a patio or windowsill,
with this easy-to-paint planter box. Bulbs can be grown in pots and
placed in the planter, just as they begin to flower. Make sure the pots
fit snugly into the box, before planting the bulbs.*

PREPARATION

In a glass jar, combine two parts All Purpose Sealer with one part water and enough Brown Earth paint to make a dark chocolate brown mix. Mix this well. This stain will keep indefinitely in a screw-top container.

Prepare the box for staining, by lightly sanding the surfaces in the direction of the grain with a sanding sponge. Wipe away the dust with a damp rag. Start on the underside of the box so you can practise the technique and test the colour. It is important to stain small sections at a time, to avoid streaks and tide lines occuring.

Dampen a small section of the box and, using the No 4 hog hair brush, paint the chocolate brown mix into the crevices. Then, with a dry rag, rub the stain onto the plank area, rubbing away any streaks as you work. If the stain is too pale, add a little more Brown Earth paint. If it is too dark, lighten it by adding more sealer and water. Do not use white paint to lighten. Move onto the next area and continue until the entire box is stained. Allow the box to dry overnight. Tape over beading around the design area with masking tape to protect it while painting the design.

TRANSFERRING THE DESIGN

Trace the Tulip Design from the pattern on page 137 onto tracing paper and then, using Saral paper and a stylus, transfer the design onto the box. At this stage, do not transfer the individual petals but only the silhouette outline of the tulips. Repeat the pattern around the box. On our box it was repeated three time across the front and back and once on each end.

PAINTING THE DESIGN

LEAVES

Mix Teal Green and Nimbus Grey in three different combinations: (4:1), (2:1) and (1:1). Using the No 3 round brush, paint leaves 1 and 2 and the stems on the two back tulips with the first mix. Paint leaves 3 to 6 with the second mix and the remaining leaves and stems with the third mix. Allow to dry.

Mix Teal Green and Carbon Black to a deep green on your palette. Shade the leaves using the 12mm (½in) flat brush dipped into retarder and side-loaded with the deep green mix. Using the step-by-step photograph on page 136 as a guide, shade the leaves where indicated by crosses on the design pattern. Allow this to dry.

Dip the brush in retarder and side-load with Warm White, mixed with a touch of Teal Green. Highlight the leaves using the photograph as a guide. Use the 12mm (½in) flat brush for large areas and the 6mm (¼in) flat brush for smaller areas. Highlight the tips of the leaves and where two leaves cross over.

Allow the paint to dry. It may be necessary to re-shade and re-highlight some leaves if the first coat is not notice-able. Always deepen the background areas that sit behind the foreground.

TULIPS

Base in all tulips with Smoked Pearl and allow to dry. Paint the tulip on the left of each clump in Burgundy. Paint the tulip to the right purple, made by mixing equal parts of Diox Purple and Warm White, with a touch of Cerulean Blue. The bud and the tallest tulip are yellow made with equal parts of Turners Yellow and Warm White, and the pink tulip on the right-hand side of the clump is painted in a mix of two parts Plum Pink to one part each of Fawn and Warm

FINISHED SIZE

- 57cm x 15½cm (22½in x 6¼in) (design only)

MATERIALS

- 55cm x 25cm x 21cm (22in x 10in x 8½in) wooden planter box
- Jo Sonja's All Purpose Sealer
- Jo Sonja's Retarder
- Glass jar with lid
- Sanding sponge
- Cloth
- 2 rags made of T-shirt material
- White Saral paper and stylus
- Tracing paper
- Masking tape (optional)
- No 4 flat-hog hair brush
- No 3 round brush
- 12mm (½in) flat brush
- 6mm (¼in) flat brush
- No 5 synthetic round brush
- Jo Sonja's Artists' Acrylics: Brown Earth, Teal Green, Nimbus Grey, Warm White, Smoked Pearl, Burgundy, Diox Purple, Turners Yellow, Plum Pink, Fawn, Raw Umber, Carbon Black
- Matisse Flow Formula: Cerulean Blue
- Easycraft satin varnish

Step-by-step guide to the painting.

White. Allow the paint to dry then re-coat. Continue adding coats, drying between each, until a solid coverage is reached.

When the paint is dry, transfer the lines of the petals from the pattern. The shading and highlighting on the tulips are painted using a dry brush technique. For a full explanation of this method, see the Techniques section at the back of this book. Use the step-by-step photograph as a guide.

Mix equal parts of Burgundy, Brown Earth and Raw Umber and allow to dry to a thick, creamy consistency on the palette. Moisten the No 5 brush then squeeze out any excess moisture. Stroke the burgundy mixture over the areas on the left-hand tulip to be shaded, using fairy-wisp strokes. Begin slowly and build

up an intensity of colour. Paint in the direction of the petals, rounding your strokes to curve on the sides and straightening them in the centre.

Using the same method as above, shade the yellow and pink tulips with a mix of equal parts of Burgundy and Brown Earth. Then shade the purple tulip with Diox Purple. Allow the shading to dry completely.

Warm White is used in the same manner to highlight all the tulips. Start on the petals at the back and work forward. Form divisions between petals, by allowing your shading colour to remain unpainted. If you happen to cover it, re-shade with your dark colour.

Allow the planter box to dry completely. It will be necessary to paint

the white highlighted areas several times. Each time you re-do the white, finish the highlighting a little nearer the top of the flower so the white is stronger on the tips of each petal. When the paint is dry, use Turners Yellow to bring some yellow highlights onto the tips of the yellow tulips.

FINISHING

When the paint is thoroughly dry, remove masking tape. If desired, re-stain the border area. Leave your work overnight and then varnish. At least four coats of varnish are necessary.

TULIP DESIGN OUTLINE

SS

Australian Bush Wreath

*By creating craft pieces with a bush theme, you are helping to further
a tradition that is unique to Australia. While this floral wreath uses
traditional appliqué and embroidery techniques practised in many countries
for decades, sometimes centuries, the native flora motifs are distinctively ours.*

PREPARATION

Photocopy each piece of the pattern on page 141, enlarging it by the amount indicated at the bottom of the page. Join the photocopied pieces together with magic tape to make the complete design. The full-sized design should form a slightly flattened circle with a diameter of about 51.5cm (20¼in). Mark the centre point of the design.

Find the centre of the background fabric by folding it in half lengthwise and then widthwise. Matching the centre points, position the background fabric on top of the photocopied design then pin the fabric in place.

Using a soft pencil, lightly trace the complete design onto the background fabric, marking just inside the design line so that the completed appliqué will cover the markings.

WORKING THE FIRST SECTION

The bush wreath is worked in four sections with one section completed at a time. Working this way, means that you will not have too many cut-out shapes to sort through as you work.

CUTTING OUT

Beginning with the shapes numbered 1 to 32 on the pattern on page 141, trace the required number of shapes onto the dull side of the freezer paper and cut them out.

With the shiny side of the freezer paper down on the right side of the fabric, iron the paper templates to your chosen fabrics, leaving space between each shape for a seam allowance. Cut out the shapes, leaving a 5mm (¼in) seam allowance around the freezer paper

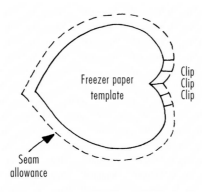

Diagram 1
Cut the fabric leaving a 5mm (¼in) allowance around the freezer paper template and clip the curves.

template. Clip the curves as shown in Diagram 1, above.

APPLIQUE THE PIECES

Pieces are sewn to the background fabric using blind stitch.

Pin the first piece (leaf 1) into place on the background fabric. With the edge of the freezer paper template as the guide, roll the seam allowance under, using the point and side of the needle to help where necessary. Roll under just a short way ahead of where you will be stitching. The seam allowance may need to be trimmed as you work.

Thread the needle with thread that closely matches the leaf fabric and tie a small knot in the end. Bring the needle from the wrong side of the background fabric, catching the folded edge of the leaf piece where you have rolled the seam allowance under. Re-enter the needle into the background fabric directly opposite where the thread has caught the folded edge. Your stitches should be small, close, firm, and at right angles to the folded edge.

Continue the appliqué work in this manner for shapes 2 to 32, sewing the shapes in place in the order of the numbers on the pattern.

FINISHED SIZE

- 55cm (21¾in) square

MATERIALS

- 58cm (23in) square of background fabric
- Assortment of blue/green print fabrics for rounded gum leaves
- Assortment of yellow/green fabrics for long gum leaves — there should be light, medium and dark values of all the green fabrics
- 20cm (8in) square of pink print fabric for gum blossoms
- 30cm (12in) square of two values of brown print fabric for gum nuts
- 3 x 15cm (6in) squares of Stitch & Tear heavy duty stabiliser
- 1m (1⅛yd) of freezer paper available at quilters' supplies shops
- Fine appliqué needles
- DMC embroidery threads for gum blossoms and veins on leaves
- Sewing threads to match appliqué fabrics
- Soft pencil
- Magic tape

NOTE: All fabrics should be 100 per cent cotton and should be washed and ironed before use.

The leaves should be appliquéd in the order given on the pattern.

To prevent puckering when embroidering the gum blossom, pin a square of heavy duty Stitch & Tear stabiliser to the wrong side of the background square directly under the gum blossoms. Using two strands of embroidery thread, embroider a circle in the centre of the open gum blossom. Taking the stitches all the way through the Stitch & Tear, stitch stamens radiating out from the centre in stem stitch and place French knots at the end. For the fine stems of the gum blossoms, work three or four rows of stem stitch next to each other. When the embroidery is finished, trim the excess Stitch & Tear, leaving in place the part where the embroidery stitches have been caught down.

If you find that some of the narrow appliquéd stems are too difficult (such as those on pieces 30 and 132), they can be stem stitched instead of appliquéd.

WORKING THE REMAINING SECTIONS

When you have completed the first section, continue working in the same manner on the next section, that is, pieces 33 to 67. Then work pieces 68 to 102 and then 103 to 136, always placing the pieces in order according to the numbers on each piece.

EMBROIDERING THE APPLIQUE

When you have sewn pieces 1 to 32 in place, embroider the veins on the leaves in stem stitch using one strand of embroidery thread. Buttonhole-stitched holes randomly placed on some of the leaves, also adds a realistic touch.

FINISHING

If you wish, you can add a border to each side of the background square and frame the piece or mount it, as the wreath in the photograph has been. Alternatively you can use the wreath pattern as the central medallion of a quilt.

Stem stitch and French knots are used to embroider the gum blossoms.

Enlarge wreath on both sides of
"A", then join the pattern together.

WREATH PATTERN

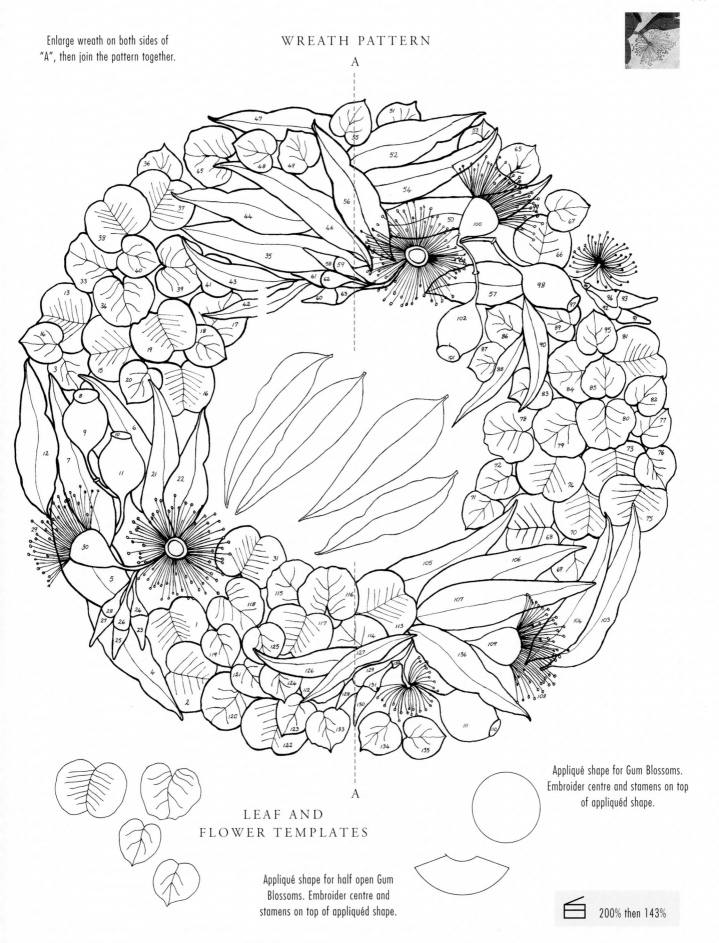

LEAF AND
FLOWER TEMPLATES

Appliqué shape for Gum Blossoms.
Embroider centre and stamens on top
of appliquéd shape.

Appliqué shape for half open Gum
Blossoms. Embroider centre and
stamens on top of appliquéd shape.

200% then 143%

Stitch Guide

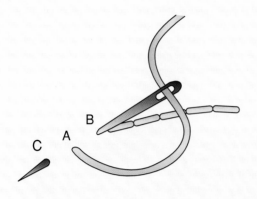

BACK STITCH

Bring the needle up at A. Take a small stitch backwards and go down at B, sliding the needle to come out at C. The distance between A and B and A and C, should be equal.

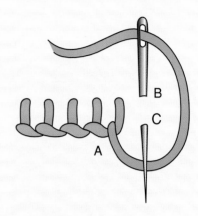

BLANKET STITCH

Working from left to right, bring the needle up at A. Hold the thread in place with your thumb, take the needle back through the fabric at B and slide it through to C, with the point of the needle over the thread. Pull the thread through and repeat, keeping the spaces between the stitches even and the vertical stitches straight.

BUTTONHOLE STITCH

This is worked the same way as blanket stitch, except the stitches are very close together. It is sometimes used for finishing scalloped edges or in cutwork. Also used for a decorative edging, with the vertical stitches alternatively worked long and short.

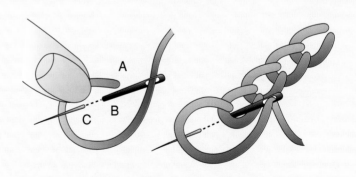

CHAIN STITCH (CONTINUOUS)

Bring the needle up at A. Slide the needle from B (as close as possible to A, but not actually through the same hole) through to C, taking the tip of the needle over the loop formed. Continue in this manner, creating a chain.

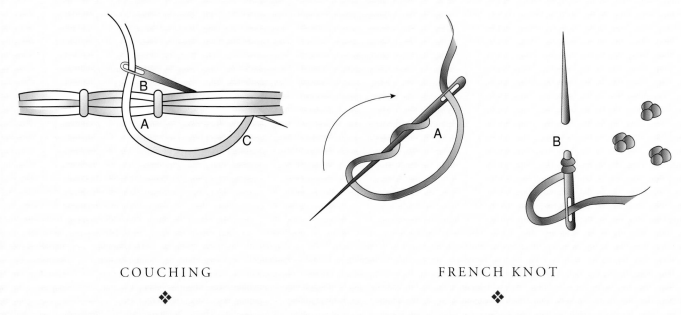

COUCHING

❖

Bring out the thread to be couched at the start of the stitching line. Remove the needle and hold the thread in place with your thumb. Thread another needle with the couching thread and bring it up on the stitching line at A. Take a small stitch over the laid thread at B, bringing the needle up again at C. Repeat to the end of the stitching line, keeping your couching stitches evenly spaced. Rethread the couched thread and take it through to the back of the work and fasten off.

FRENCH KNOT

❖

Bring the needle up at A and wrap the thread around the needle the specified number of times. Holding the thread firmly, go down at B (as close as possible to A without actually going through the same hole). The knot should be held in place while the needle and thread are pulled completely through to the back of the fabric.

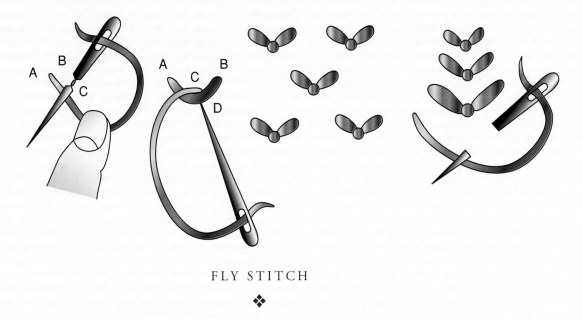

FLY STITCH

❖

Bring the needle up at A and down at B (to the right of and level with A), coming up again at C, with the tip of the needle over the thread. Pull the thread through the fabric and go to the back of the work again at D. This stitch can be used singly or stacked one on top of the other.

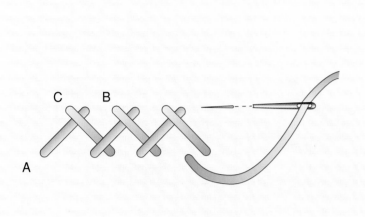

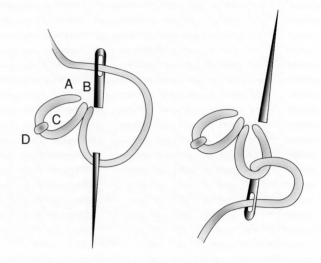

HERRINGBONE STITCH

❖

Work from left to right. Bring the needle up at A and insert at B, sliding the needle behind the fabric to come out again at C (forming a small, horizontal Back Stitch). Continue working from side to side.

LAZY DAISY (DETACHED CHAIN)

❖

Bring the needle up at A. Slide the needle from B (as close as possible to A, but not actually through the same hole) through to C, taking the tip of the needle over the loop formed. Go down at D, creating a holding stitch.

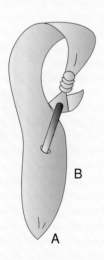

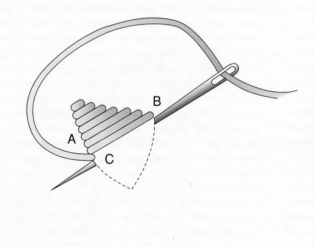

RIBBON STITCH

❖

Bring the needle up at A and lay the ribbon flat on the fabric. Put the needle into the middle of the ribbon at B and pull carefully through the fabric, making the edges of the ribbon curl towards the tip. Do not pull too tightly.

SATIN STITCH

❖

Bring the needle up at A, go down at B and slide the needle through to C. Keep working in this manner, keeping the stitches parallel and close together until the shape has been filled.

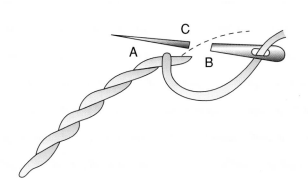

STEM STITCH: THREAD DOWN

❖

Work from the left to the right. Keeping the thread below the needle, come up at A and go back down into the fabric at B, coming out again at C (which should be halfway along the length of the previous stitch).

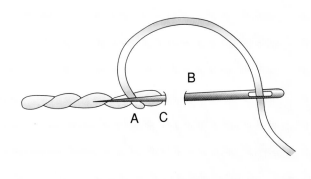

STEM STITCH: THREAD UP

❖

Work from the left to the right. Keep the thread above the needle, come up at A and go back down into the fabric at B, coming out again at C (which should be halfway along the length of the previous stitch).

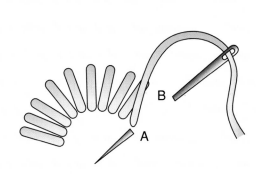

STRAIGHT STITCH

❖

Bring the needle up at A, go down again at B. Straight Stitches should be fairly firm so that they lie flat on the fabric and not too long or they may catch. They can be worked in any direction and in various lengths.

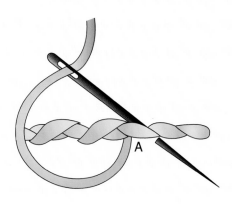

WHIPPED STEM STITCH

❖

Refer to stem stitch instructions. To whip, bring the needle up at A, take the thread over the first stitch and back under the next. Continue taking the thread over and under the stem stitches, taking care not to go through the fabric. A tapestry needle is useful for whipping.

Basic Techniques

Transferring Patterns onto Fabric

For many of the projects in this book you will need to transfer the master pattern supplied, onto your fabric. There are several simple methods you can use to achieve this.

MAKING A WORKING PATTERN

The first step in transferring your design to your fabric, is to make a working pattern from the original, master pattern in the book. The easiest way to do this is by photocopying. First check the coding on the pattern to find out if it needs enlarging and then set the photocopier to the correct percentage (leave it on 100% if the pattern is already full-size).

You can, if you prefer, trace the pattern onto tracing or greaseproof paper using a sharp pencil or a fine-tip marker. Before tracing, make sure the pattern from which you are tracing is shown full size.

TRANSFERRING THE DESIGN

There are several ways to transfer the design from the working pattern onto your fabric. It depends on the type of fabric you are using and how you will sew the design.

DIRECT TRACING

If your fabric is transparent or semi-transparent, you can place your design under the fabric and trace it directly onto the fabric. For semi-transparent materials, tape the fabric and working pattern to a window so the light will shine through, making the pattern easier to see. If your fabric is washable, trace the design with a water-soluble marker pen. If it isn't, use a fade-out pen, which will disappear from the fabric in about 48 hours. Make sure it will fade by testing the pen on a scrap of your fabric, before transferring the design.

DRESSMAKER'S CARBON

Dressmaker's carbon is an easy way to transfer designs onto non-see-through fabrics. The only disadvantage is that the carbon can be difficult to remove and should only be used when the design is to be covered with stitching. Dressmaker's carbon comes in several colours so choose one that will show up on your fabric. On a hard, flat surface place the fabric, right side up, with the working pattern on top and, using masking tape, secure the two layers to the surface at each corner. Slip the carbon between the fabric and the pattern and draw over the design lines, using a stylus or an empty ballpoint pen.

TRANSFER PENCIL

Some transfer pencils are sold as water-soluble, but test them on your fabric before you use them. Trace your design onto tracing paper then turn the design over and trace over the lines with the transfer pencil. Place the tracing paper, transfer pencil-side down, on the right side of the fabric and fix it in place with masking tape. Press down on the paper for a few minutes with a warm iron. When moving the iron to a new part of the design, lift it and replace it, do not slide the iron over the design.

PRICKING OUT

You can prick out simple designs by machine or by hand. Place your working pattern on top of the fabric and pin it into place. Place the pattern and fabric on a thick wad of fabric, such as a blanket and prick holes through the design and fabric with a needle. Using a fabric marker or fade-out pen, mark dots on the fabric though the needle holes. Remove the pattern and join up the dots. Alternatively, remove the top and bottom thread from a sewing machine and 'sew' around the design. Remove the pattern and join up the dots with a fabric marker.

The Basics of Appliqué

Appliqué, the process of applying a piece of fabric to a background, is not a difficult technique, but basic rules do apply.

FABRIC SELECTION

Cotton fabrics are preferable for appliqué because they can be creased to form a seam allowance. Weights of all fabrics should be compatible and, if the piece is to be laundered, it is a good idea to pre-wash your fabrics.

When choosing colours and patterns to include in an appliqué piece, be guided by your personal preferences. While strong colours work well in highlighting the motifs, strong patterns can also contribute to the design. Stripes, spots, flowers and geometric prints, for example, can all add dimension and vibrancy. Snip samples of fabric and place them on your background fabric, move them around to find the most pleasing juxtaposition of one contrast in relation to another. If you are using several colours in a design, cut out some of the pieces for the motifs and pin them in place to consider their suitability before you begin stitching.

TRANSFERRING THE DESIGN

Make a working pattern by photocopying the master pattern, checking first to see whether you need to enlarge it to full size. If your design is reasonably complicated, it will make the appliqué pieces easier to place correctly if you transfer the appliqué design from the working pattern onto the background fabric.

(See the previous section 'Transferring Patterns Onto Fabric' on page 146 for the best method for doing this.)

Photocopy each appliqué pattern piece, again checking whether you need to enlarge. Following the method given in the instructions for your chosen project, make all the templates needed to cut out the fabric pieces.

PREPARING THE APPLIQUE PIECES

Before the appliqué pieces are stitched onto the background fabric, they must be cut out and the raw edges turned under. There are various ways of doing this, and the designers of the projects in this book have each described their preferred method. However, you may find one of the following methods will achieve equally satisfying results for you.

BASTING

Turn the raw edges under and baste around the shape with a running stitch and light-coloured thread, beginning from the right side.

MACHINE TURNING LINE

Stitch around the pattern design outline using a matching thread and a small stitch. This line is then used as a guide for turning under the seam allowance.

GATHERING STITCH

If edges of the design are curved or rounded, work a gathering stitch around the edges then place a light cardboard template on the wrong side of the fabric and pull in the gathering to fit the shape. Always press with a hot iron to set the seam allowance.

FABRIC STARCH

Spray the fabric to be used for appliqué with fabric starch. Iron flat, transfer the design to the fabric, add the seam allowance and cut out. Place a cardboard or plastic template on the back of the fabric, iron again and finger-press the edges around the template.

FUSIBLE WEBBING

Iron fusible webbing to the back of the fabric. Trace the design, add the seam allowance and cut out. Remove the paper backing from the webbing, carefully turn edges and press them to the webbing.

FREEZER PAPER

Trace the pattern design without seam allowances, onto the dull side of freezer paper, purchased from a sewing supplier and cut out the templates. These templates can be applied in three different ways, the choice is up to you.

The first is to position the cut-out freezer paper template shiny-side down, on the wrong side of the fabric. Press with a hot iron to temporarily fuse the fabric and template, and then cut out the applique piece adding a 5mm (¼in) seam allowance. Fold the edge of the fabric over the freezer paper and press to get a sharp edge.

Alternatively, you can position the template shiny-side down on the right side of the fabric and crease and fold the raw edge behind the design.

A third way is to position the template shiny-side up (a dab of fabric glue will hold it in place) on the wrong side of the pre-cut fabric. Fold the raw edges over on to the shiny side of the freezer paper and carefully press the edge with a hot iron to temporarily fuse the seam allowance. Position this on the background fabric and iron it again to hold the piece in place ready for stitching.

NON-WOVEN INTERFACING

Cut out the design from the fabric, including a 5mm (¼in) seam allowance and place it right side down on a piece of lightweight interfacing. Stitch around the design outline, either with small hand stitches or machine stitching. Re-cut the interfaced design including the 5mm (¼in) seam allowance. Cut a small slit in the back of the interfacing and turn the design right side out. The raw edge turnings are now all inside the design.

ATTACHING THE APPLIQUE

HAND STITCHING METHOD

To hand appliqué without the stitches showing is the goal of nearly every appliquér. Hem stitch (also known as slip stitch), or ladder stitch can be used to appliqué the designs. Cut a 40cm length of thread and make a small knot. Making sure the knot sits underneath the piece being appliqued, bring the thread from the back through the background fabric and catch a couple of threads on the applique piece. Continue to stitch, making sure that the needle enters the background fabric directly opposite where it came out on the top piece and slightly under the piece being appliquéd. When you have

completed stitching, finish off on the back with a couple of small back stitches.

Hand appliqué can be worked in hem stitch or ladder stitch.

MACHINE STITCHING METHOD

For invisible machine work, use normal thread that matches the background fabric in the bobbin and monofilament thread on top. Smoke-coloured thread should be used for dark fabrics and clear thread for light fabrics.

Use a straight stitch just inside the outline of the piece, then cover the stitching line with a zigzag set close enough to create a satin stitch finish. Alternatively, set the machine to a blind hem stitch and sew alongside the design, positioning the needle so the stitches are placed just outside the edge of the motif to give a neat appearance.

A sheet of unwaxed greaseproof paper placed behind the background fabric when stitching, will provide stability and prevent the work from stretching and puckering out of shape.

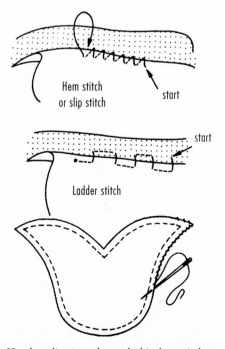

Hand appliqué can be worked in hem stitch or ladder stitch

The Basics of Cross-Stitching

Counted cross-stitch is an easy stitch to work and with just a little bit of practice, the basic technique can be quickly mastered.

FABRIC

Counted thread embroidery is done on fabric that is woven with the same number of vertical and horizontal threads per inch. The fineness or coarseness of the fabric is called its count and this is measured by the number of threads per inch (2.5cm). For example, 18 count has 18 threads to the inch while 11 count has 11 threads to the inch. The count of the fabric determines the size of the design after it has been worked. A design worked on an 18 count fabric will be considerably smaller than one which is stitched on an 11 count fabric.

PREPARING THE FABRIC

If your finished cross-stitch is going to be washed at any time in the future, test the fabric for possible shrinkage. Cut a small 6cm (2⅜in) square of fabric and draw around it on a sheet of paper. Wash, dry and press the square and then place it on the drawn square. If the piece has shrunk, place the rest of the fabric in hot water, let it dry and then press.

Bind the edges of the fabric before you begin stitching, to prevent fraying. This can be done using an overlocker or by machine-sewing a row of zigzag close to the raw edge. Or you can overcast the edge by hand or bind it with masking tape, which will come off easily without damaging the fabric threads.

Before you start sewing, make sure your fabric is straight by laying it on a flat surface and placing a set square at each corner. The edges of the fabric should follow those of the set square. If they do not, pull the fabric gently at a 45 degree angle to the weave, until the piece is straight. A little steam from an iron may help with this in difficult cases.

WORKING THE DESIGN

Each square on a cross-stitch chart represents one complete cross-stitch, or a space equal to the size of a stitch. No matter how many fabric threads the cross stitch is worked over, it is always represented by only one square on the chart.

Marking the centre of your fabric.

Cross-stitch designs are normally started from the centre and worked out towards the edges. This ensures the design is positioned correctly and you

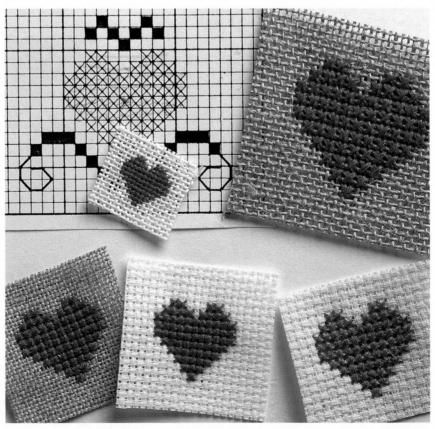

The size of the work depends on the fabric you select.

don't run out of space. Find the centre of the fabric by working a line of running stitches from the halfway point on the top edge, down to the bottom edge and between the halfway points on the sides. With the centre point established and these guidelines clearly visible, you can begin plotting the design from the cross stitch chart. Where a motif appears in isolation, it may be easier to mark its position using tacking thread or a water-soluble marking pen.

PREPARING THREADS

Cut your thread to a maximum length of between 45cm (18in) and 60cm (24in). A thread much shorter than this will fray and a thread too long is uncomfortable to work with and can also knot, twist or fray. If you are using stranded embroidery cotton, separate it into single strands and then re-form with one or more strands to the thickness required. The number of strands depends on the count of the fabric and how much coverage you want. The general rule is to use six strands for 6 count fabric, three or four strands for 11 count, two or three strands for 14 count, one or two strands for 18 count and one strand for 22 count fabric or above.

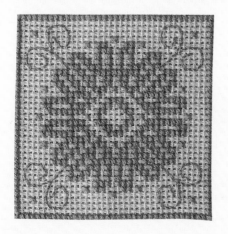

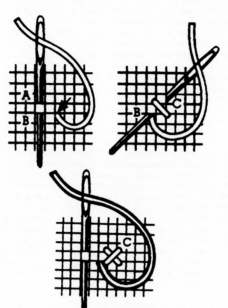

Working one stitch at a time.

STARTING OFF

It is best not to begin your work with a knot on the wrong side because it can make a bump visible on the right side, or can pull through the work after you have started stitching. There are several methods that can be used instead. The easiest is to work one or two back stitches on the wrong side just before the starting point, to anchor the thread securely and then continue stitching until you have covered the back stitches. If some stitches have already been worked in the area, you can fasten the new thread by back-stitching it to the underside of the existing stitches.

To finish a thread, simply run it through a few stitches on the wrong side and anchor it with a back stitch or two. Do not carry threads across long distances on the wrong side. Depending on the weight of the fabric and the colour of the thread, such jumps may be visible. As a general rule, avoid jumps longer than 1¼cm (½in) in length.

STITCHING

Cross-stitches can be worked one stitch at a time, which produces the most even effect, or they can be worked in two journeys, which is a quicker way of covering large areas. This second method also uses slightly less thread and helps to ensure that all the stitches slant the same way. Whichever method you use, make sure that the top diagonal of all stitches in the design slant the same way.

WORKING CROSS-STITCH IN A ROW

If you are working on a multi-coloured design you might find it more convenient to use several colours at once rather than fastening off small amounts. One way of doing this is to take the threaded needle out of the way of the stitching on the right side, inserting it into the fabric temporarily, and threading a second needle with the next colour. Another way is to use just one needle, rethreading it with the different colours as required and pinning the discontinued threads out of the way on the right side of the fabric.

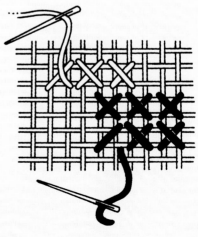

Working a multicoloured design.

The Basics of Folk Art

While folk art techniques are not difficult, it takes practice to achieve the simple, spontaneous look of this craft.

PREPARING SURFACES

Sand all raw wood surfaces and seal before decorating. Use an all-purpose clear sealer, thinned with water for a raw wood look, or use two or more coats of special purpose basecoat, with sealer already in it. Previously painted or varnished wood should be sanded before sealing. Do not apply sealer to Australian craftwood, as it will create a barrier that will hinder the absorption of the paint.

Coat glass or plastic with undiluted sealer and allow it to dry hard. With terracotta, the use of sealer will depend on the finish you require. Base paint can be painted on directly, and two coats are usually needed. However, if you wish to retain the terracotta colour, apply one coat of a 2:1 mix of sealer and water and sand it lightly when dry. This will give the terracotta a shiny appearance. If you like the look of terracotta just as it is, trace your design directly onto the pot and paint. Finish the pot with a matt varnish to retain this appearance.

BASECOATING

A basecoat is usually applied before the design, unless you intend the original surface to be seen behind the pattern. Rather than dipping the brush straight into the basecoat container, place a small amount of paint on a tile, palette or plastic plate and replenish it when necessary. If you wash the brush between coats, use clean water and dry the brush before recommencing painting.

Apply the paint in long strokes, working towards the sides, smoothing any ridges of paint away immediately. If you are having difficulty achieving a smooth texture in your paint, try using flow medium instead of water to thin it.

Normally two coats are needed, as the first coat does not give a solid coverage. It is best not to overwork the paint in an attempt to cover in one coat. Instead, allow the first coat to dry and sand lightly following the grain. If painting on craftwood, a light sanding on the flat surface will be sufficient. Continue to paint and sand lightly between coats, until a solid coverage is reached. Lightly sand once more before applying the design.

TRANSFERRING THE DESIGN

Set your working pattern in place on the object you are going to paint, securing it at the corners with masking tape which can easily be removed without marking the surface.

Under the working pattern, slip transfer paper, which comes in various colours and can be purchased from artists' suppliers. Never use ordinary carbon paper. Using light pressure, trace over the design with a stylus or ballpoint pen. If you need to, you can remove lines later with an eraser.

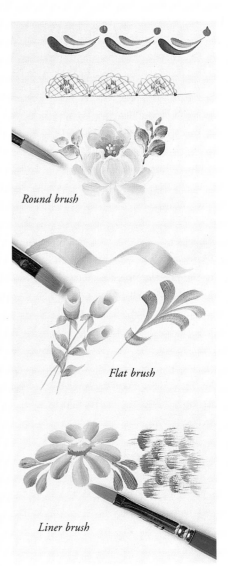

Round brush

Flat brush

Liner brush

BRUSHES

Both round and flat brushes, which come in various sizes, are used in folk art together with liner brushes for executing fine line work. A round brush is the most commonly used brush as it can be used for many purposes, from fine lace work to large dry brushed designs. Sizes 2,3,4 and 5 are the most useful. Flat brushes are flat and rectangular shaped and come in different lengths. The shader brush is medium length and the most versatile, while the blender is shorter and a little easier to use. The angle shader has the end of the hairs cut diagonally, which makes painting in tight corners easier.

BRUSH STROKES

COMMA STROKE

The comma stroke is the basic stroke used in folk art. Load a round brush with slightly thinned paint and roll to a good point. Carefully pick up some thick paint on the tip of the brush. Hold the brush vertically as you press down on the paper. Pause to allow the hairs to fan out, then gradually pull the brush towards you, releasing pressure and lifting simultaneously. Complete the comma stroke by bringing the brush back to a point and making a fine tail.

'S' STROKE

The S stroke is made by touching the paper with the loaded brush, tip only, then gradually applying pressure while pulling in an S shape. Then lift to return to a fine point.

SCALLOPED STROKE

Hold a well-loaded brush at a 45 degree angle. Apply pressure and lift, while pulling in a line to create a scalloped top and a flat base.

DOTS

Dots can be easily created by dipping a brush end or stylus into thick paint and then using it like a stamp. By dipping the brush in once and making several dots, each will get gradually smaller. For even rows of dots, re-dip the tool every third or fourth dot.

SIDE-LOADING

Load the brush with the main colour you want to use, then gradually pull the brush through a second colour. This will make a stripe along one side of the brush only, but be careful to avoid wetting the tip. By gently rolling the brush towards the contrast colour, a thicker edge of colour contrast can then be created.

DOUBLE-LOADING

Double-loading is achieved by loading the brush fully with just one colour, then stroking the tip through a contrast colour. This creates a streaky effect of one colour pulling through into the next.

DRY BRUSHING

Onto a dry, flat brush, load a creamy paint, then blot on a paper towel to remove any excess. Using a very light touch, glide the paint over the surface, giving a textured look to the stroke. Build up strength very gradually, or it can become blotchy.

SHADING

To achieve a shaded effect, load a large flat brush with either flow medium or water and blot both sides till the shine has gone. Dip one corner of the brush into the paint and blend both sides of the brush well. The colour should graduate evenly from full colour to nothing, with no harsh line at the colour edge. The larger the brush, the greater the blending area. Remember, the size of the float depends on the amount of paint, and not on the size of the brush you are using.

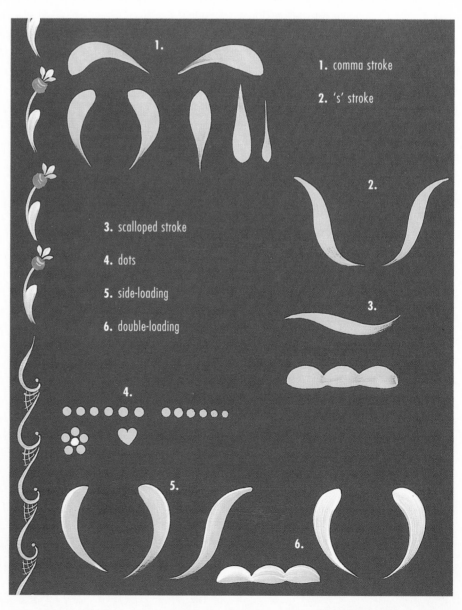

1. comma stroke

2. 's' stroke

3. scalloped stroke

4. dots

5. side-loading

6. double-loading

The Basics of Floral Arranging

There are no rules for putting a floral design together, but there are a few hints and basic guidelines that will help. Both container and plant material need to be considered together to achieve a harmonious design. Careful preparation and an eye for structure are important factors in successful flower arranging.

PREPARING THE CONTAINER

❖

The right choice of container is important to the overall effect and is a key factor in the arrangement. A container may be the inspiration and focal point for an arrangement.

Before you begin, ensure your container is clean because any leftover leaves or debris stuck to the side, or dried residue from dirty water can harbour bacteria which can spoil the arrangement. Long tall vases that are difficult to reach into, can be cleaned by swirling a tablespoon or two of bleach in a little water around the vase. Rinse the container several times with fresh cold water to clear the bleach.

Floral foam, or oasis, is a versatile device for securing flowers in a vase as it can be cut to fit any shape or size. Before inserting the oasis, soak it in water for no more than an hour as over-soaked floral foam becomes crumbly. If you intend inserting long or thick stems into the foam, wrap a layer of mesh around the block to help hold it together. Foam needs to be anchored to the bottom of the container to prevent it floating to the top. It can be anchored with either a heavyweight pin holder or one or more plastic pronged holders hot-glued to the

Attractive floral wreaths can be made in just about any shape you can imagine.

bottom or attached with plasticine. Alternatively, place a grid of floral tape over the mouth of the container. Extend the tape ends over the edge of the vase and secure with a circle of extra tape. Floral foam can be purchased as a kit with its own container containing a plastic guard that is placed over the foam and snapped into custom-made holes.

Floral foam, both fresh and dried, should be cut big enough to take the plant stems. Allow some room for topping up with water but be careful not to cut it too small. To achieve a flowing

design in shallow containers, the floral foam should extend 1cm (³⁄₈in) above the rim of the container, plant material can be placed into the sides.

SORTING THE PLANT MATERIAL

Sort the plant material into groups so you can clearly see what and how much there is. Group types and colours together, then experiment to see what pleases your eye most by lying or holding the groups beside each other. Seeing it this way helps you to establish balance and shape. When arranging into floral foam, stems need to be clean and free of nubbles, thorns, leaves and pokey bits. The stem should be inserted about 2–3cm (1in) into the foam, and should be cleanly cut, not broken.

Remove all leaves and foliage below the waterline. Submerged leaves spoil the water, rot quickly, are smelly and detract from the design. The water is part of the whole arrangement in a clear glass container and its clean appearance is important. Water should be changed or topped up regularly.

PUTTING IT TOGETHER

Have a rubbish bin or box handy for any clippings and try to keep the area surrounding your arrangement clear, so you are not reaching over or around cut stems and debris to place your material into your design.

The most common and easiest way of making a start to your design is to begin with a framework of foliage to set the outline, shape and limits of the arrangement. Place the foliage securely in the container, aiming for a 3-dimensional look.

Once the framework is established and the shape pleases your eye, follow through with the flowers to strengthen the shape. In building the flowers through your arrangement, they should be both projected and recessed, to give a feeling of depth and to avoid a 'flat' look. This is easily achieved by cutting your flowers to different lengths and placing them at different heights and angles. Avoid crossed stems.

Try to avoid mirror images. Flowers are seldom exactly the same in shape and form and a better balance is achieved by complementary sides rather than attempting to match or twin each side. Generally, odd numbers are more aesthetically pleasing in an arrangement than even numbers. Darker colours should be kept more towards the centre or bottom to give a focal point, and lighter colours towards the outside.

Remember, there really are no rules, just guidelines, and flower arranging is not a competition to use everything in sight. Simply put some flowers together in the colours you love, treat them carefully and have fun.

The Basics of Quilting

Patience and the mastery of a few basic techniques are essentials of quilt making. Choice of fabric and accurate cutting and assembly of blocks are essential.

FABRIC

Some fabrics are easier to work with than others. The easiest to use is a firmly woven, lightweight, 100 per cent cotton fabric which also lasts longer and gives crisper results. If using synthetics or synthetic mixes, make sure they are easy to iron, do not crush too easily and will not pucker when sewn. Avoid satins and taffeta, as they are too fragile for patchwork. Stretch, heavy or closely woven fabrics should also be avoided. It is a good idea before you start, to sew a few test pieces to make sure you are happy with the fabric's qualities.

Much of the art of patchwork is in the choice of colours. The value of the colour, its lightness or darkness, is often more important than the actual colour, and the best results are achieved by using a variety of values. Experiment with prints of varying scale and motif, but be careful with stripes. If they are not cut and sewn perfectly straight, it will be very obvious.

Always wash new fabrics before use to pre-shrink them and to remove the sizing and any excess dye. Machine-washing is more effective than hand-washing for this task. Iron the washed fabrics while they are still damp.

TEMPLATES

Photocopy the pattern to the correct size and trace the template accurately onto template plastic with the aid of a ruler. If you are machine sewing the blocks, add a 5mm (¼in) seam allowance right around the template, unless this is already

indicated on the pattern. If hand-sewing, you can add the seam allowance when you cut out the fabric. Transfer any markings on the pattern to the template.

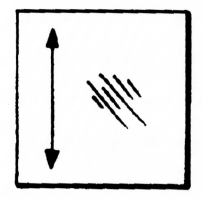

Standard template (handsewing)

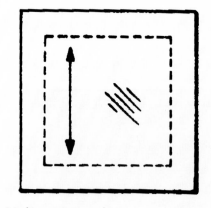

Machine sewing template

CUTTING

Trim the selvedge from the fabric before cutting and, if you are using the same fabric for both borders and some of the block pieces, cut the borders first and use what is left over for the block pieces.

Position the templates on your fabric so the arrows match the straight grain of the fabric. With a sharp pencil or pen, trace around the template onto the fabric.

If a seam allowance was added to the template for machine-sewing, cut the fabric carefully along the marked line. If the fabric is to be hand-sewing, cut 5mm (¼in) outside the lines.

Multiple layers can be cut at the one time by folding and pressing your fabric into layers, before laying the template on. Remember to make sure that each piece is cut on the straight grain.

PIECING

Follow the instructions on the pattern to determine which pieces are to be joined together and in what order. Pin the adjoining pieces together, right sides facing and sew using either the hand-piecing or the machine-piecing method below.

HAND PIECING

Sew the seam through the pencilled lines with a short running stitch and occasional back stitch, using a single thread. Begin and end each seam at the seam line (not at the edge of fabric) with two or three back stitches, to secure the seam.

When joining blocks and rows together do not sew the seam allowance down. Instead, sew right up to the dot marking the corner and then begin on the next side by again taking a couple of small back stitches before continuing. By doing this, you leave your options open as to which way you choose to press the seam allowance when the block is completed.

MACHINE PIECING

Use white or neutral thread as light in colour as the lightest colour in the project. Use a dark neutral thread for piecing dark solids.

Align cut edges of the patches with the edge of the presser foot if it is 5mm (¼in) wide. If not, place masking tape on the throat plate of the machine 5mm (¼in) away from the needle, to

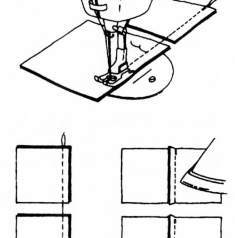

Machine piecing

guide you. Sew all the way to the cut edge, unless you are inserting a patch into an angle. Short seams need not be pinned unless matching is involved. Keep pins away from the seam line.

Use chain piecing whenever possible to save time and thread. To chain piece, sew one seam, but do not lift the presser foot. Do not take the piece out of the sewing machine and do not cut the thread. Instead, set up the next piece to be sewn and continue stitching. There will be little twists of thread between the two pieces. Sew all the seams you can at one time in this way, then remove the 'chain', and clip the threads. When joining rows, make sure matching seam allowances are pressed in opposite directions to reduce bulk and make matching easier. Pin pieces together directly through the stitching and to the right or left of the seam, remove pins as you sew.

then four, and so on, until the top is completed. Press all allowances in one direction, either up or down.

BLOCKS JOINED WITH VERTICAL AND HORIZONTAL SASHINGS

Join the blocks into strips with a vertical sash between each pair of blocks. Sew a horizontal piece of sashing to each strip, then join the strips to form the quilt top.

QUILTING

Lay the backing material, right side down on a hard, flat surface, pulling it taut and fixing the corners with masking tape. Lay the batting on top, smoothing it to get rid of any wrinkles. Place the top layer, right side up over the batting. Pin through all three layers and then baste the three layers together around the edge — in a diagonal pattern through the centre and then in a large grid pattern over the whole quilt. This will hold the pieces securely while you quilt.

Work out your quilting pattern and transfer it to a paper pattern.

Lightly mark the design onto the quilt top, using a water-soluble marker pen or pencil. (Be sure to test water-soluble pens for removability before marking the quilt.) Mark dark-coloured fabrics with a chalk pencil. Some quilting may be done without marking the top.

Outline quilting, and quilting in the ditch, can be done by 'marking' the sewing line by eye. In outline quilting, lines are sewn 5mm (¼in) from the seams around the patches, while in quilting in the ditch, the sewing line is placed right next to the seam on the side without the seam allowances. Other straight lines may be marked as you quilt, by using a piece of masking tape that can be pulled away after the line is quilted along its edge.

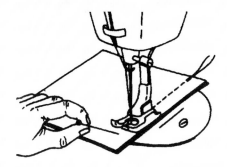

JOINING THE BLOCKS

Depending on the design, blocks are joined to each other or with sashing between them.

BLOCKS JOINED EDGE - TO - EDGE

Join the blocks to form strips the width of the quilt. Working one strip at a time, first pin each seam very carefully, inserting a pin at right angles to the seam wherever seams meet. Stitch using a 5mm ¼in seam allowance. Join all rows in this manner. Press all seam allowances in the odd-numbered rows in one direction and all seam allowances in even numbered rows in the opposite direction.

To join the rows, first pin two rows together so that seam lines match up perfectly. Join rows in groups of two,

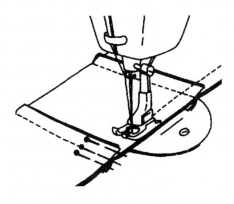

Joining the blocks into strips.

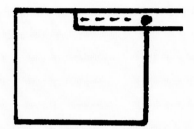

Stop 12mm (½in) from the corner, back stitch to secure and take the quilt out of machine.

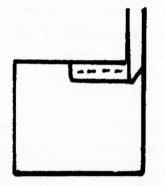

Fold the binding up making a 45 degree angle with the binding strip.

Fold down level with the edge and sew to the next corner and repeat.

Quilting is done in a short running stitch, with a single strand of thread that goes through all three layers. Use a short needle (8 or 9 betweens) with about 45cm (18in) of thread. Make a small knot in the thread and take a first long stitch about 2.5cm (1in) through the top and batting only, coming up where the quilting will begin. Tug on the thread to pull the knotted end between the layers. Take straight, even stitches that are the same size on the top and bottom of the quilt. To end a line of quilting, take a tiny back stitch, make another small knot and pull between the layers. Make another inch-long stitch through the top and the batting only and clip the thread

at the surface of the quilt. Carefully pull out the basting threads when all the quilting is finished.

BINDING

Trim the edges of the quilt and cut the binding fabric into strips, selvedge to selvedge. Join the strips to make one long strip. Alternatively, to make continuous binding, cut your strip along the bias or diagonal grain. Iron it in half along the length, wrong sides together. Sew to the quilt top, starting at the centre

bottom, 12mm (½in) from the raw edges. To mitre the binding, stop 12mm (½in) from the corner, back stitch to secure and take the quilt out of machine. Fold the binding up making a 45 degree angle with the binding strip. Fold down level with the edge and sew to the next corner. Repeat and overlap the ends of the binding. Slip stitch in place to the back of the quilt. A nice finishing touch is to embroider your name, city and date on the back of the quilt.

Index

Projects are in italics

Country Decorating

The arrival of *Australian Country Craft & Decorating* magazine in 1991 signalled the beginning of a new era in craftin this country. The magazine's superb photographic features, polished editorial and meticulously researched projects have helped elevate craft from the relative obscurity of a cottage industry to the magnitude of a multi-million dollar industry.

Australian Country Craft & Decorating continues to raise the profile of craft and craftspeople in Australia. It has been the catalyst for a number of other craft publications and virtually all of them
have been unbridled successes.

Australian Country Craft & Decorating is without doubt the leading magazine of its type in Australia. Locally, its popularity is ever-increasing and it has gained a reputation overseas as a publication of quality. Quite simply, if your interest lies in craft or the decorative arts *Australian Country Craft & Decorating* magazine is essential reading.